O9-ABF-371

# Longevity Policy

HD
7125
.T849
2011

# Longevity Policy

## Facing Up to Longevity Issues Affecting Social Security, Pensions, and Older Workers

John A. Turner

2011

W.E. Upjohn Institute for Employment Research
Kalamazoo, Michigan

KVCC KALAMAZOO VALLEY COMMUNITY COLLEGE LIBRARY

**Library of Congress Cataloging-in-Publication Data**


Turner, John A. (John Andrew), 1949 July 9–
  Longevity policy : facing up to longevity issues affecting social security, pensions, and older workers / John A. Turner.
    p. cm.
  Includes bibliographical references and index.
  ISBN-13: 978-0-88099-377-7 (pbk. : alk. paper)
  ISBN-10: 0-88099-377-4 (pbk. : alk. paper)
  ISBN-13: 978-0-88099-378-4 (hbk. : alk. paper)
  ISBN-10: 0-88099-378-2 (hbk: alk. paper)
  1. Social security—United States. 2. Pensions—Government policy—United States.
3. Older people—Employment—Government policy—United States. I. Title.
  HD7125.T849 2011
  368.4'300973—dc23
                                2011022673

© 2011
W.E. Upjohn Institute for Employment Research
300 S. Westnedge Avenue
Kalamazoo, Michigan 49007-4686

The facts presented in this study and the observations and viewpoints expressed are the sole responsibility of the author. They do not necessarily represent positions of the W.E. Upjohn Institute for Employment Research.

Cover design by Alcorn Publication Design.
Index prepared by Diane Worden.
Printed in the United States of America.
Printed on recycled paper.

KALAMAZOO VALLEY
COMMUNITY COLLEGE
LIBRARY

# Contents

# Tables

# Acknowledgments

I have greatly benefited from collaboration with distinguished coauthors, whose work with me I have cited and to whom I express gratitude: Clive Bailey, Daniel Beller, Yung-Ping Chen, Teresa Ghilarducci, Colin Gillion, Roy Guenther, Mark Iwry, Denis Latulippe, Courtney Monk, Dana Muir, Christian Toft, Satyendra Verma, Hazel Witte, and Natalia Zhivan. I have received valuable comments from Kevin Hollenbeck, Benjamin Jones, and three anonymous reviewers. I wish to thank my wife, Kathy, and daughter, Sarah, for supporting my absences to write, attend conferences, and work abroad. I thank my parents, Henry and Mary, for ultimately making everything possible.

# 1

# The Policy Challenges of Increasing Longevity

## Paying the Costs of Living Longer

Increases in life expectancy are no secret, yet government policy does not explicitly deal with their well-known consequences for Social Security financing. Every day 12,000 baby boomers turn 50. Continuing improvements in life expectancy mean that those people will live longer on average than any previous generation. That fortunate development, however, poses public policy challenges as to how to pay for the living costs of those added years.

This book focuses on public policy issues concerning Social Security, pensions, and older workers that arise because people are living longer. The question it addresses is, "What should be the retirement policy responses to increased longevity?" Not only has increased longevity occurred for all major demographic groups, but people are healthier at older ages. This book draws on international experience to recommend solutions for U.S. policy.

The premise of the book is that public policy should recognize longevity policy as a distinct area—as we do now, for example, for climate change. The reason longevity policy is best treated as a unified policy area is that the challenges arising from increased longevity are best dealt with when the interrelationships between work at older ages, Social Security, and pensions are recognized. Rather than separately treating the issues raised by life expectancy in policies toward older workers, and in other unrelated policies concerning Social Security and pensions, a unified approach toward policies concerning Social Security, pensions, and work at older ages would facilitate making needed changes in each of the areas. Because of interconnections between these three areas, policy will be more effective if it considers them together, rather than separately. Furthermore, the book argues that policy should be developed that is directly related to the effects of increasing life expectancy.

Social Security is projected to have insufficient funding to pay promised benefits on time. The 2011 report of the trustees of Social Security projects that Social Security will not have sufficient resources to pay benefits on time starting in 2036, at which point it will be able to pay 75 percent of promised benefits. The annual cost of Social Security benefits represented 4.8 percent of GDP in 2009 and is projected to increase gradually to 6.1 percent of GDP in 2035 and then decline to about 5.9 percent of GDP by 2050 and remain at about that level. The projected 75-year actuarial deficit for the combined Old-Age and Survivors Insurance and Disability Insurance (OASI and DI) Trust Funds is 1.92 percent of taxable payroll (Social Security Board of Trustees 2011).

When Social Security is reformed to deal with its financing insufficiency, the effects of the changes will depend on whether employers and workers extend work at older ages and what changes are made to pensions provided by employers. Features of Social Security affect when people retire, but so do pensions and labor market conditions. Living longer affects all three areas, so that policy dealing with greater life expectancy should address all three areas at the same time.

Many of our social policies and employee benefit policies were designed for an era when people had shorter lives. With the demographic changes occurring, it is time to reexamine those policies so that they fit the realities of the new demographic era of living longer.

## LIFE-EXPECTANCY INCREASES

### Overall Gains and Distributional Issues

The policies proposed in this book are specifically designed to address the effects of life-expectancy increases. Thus, as a starting point, it is important to understand something about those increases. In the past 50 years, the increase in life expectancy at older ages has been considerable. Life expectancy at age 65 rose from 14.4 years in 1960 to 18.5 years in 2006, an increase of four years (Arias et al. 2008). This change has considerably increased the cost of providing pensions.

Yet the full story is more complex than simply one of widespread increases in life expectancy. The United States has a diverse population in terms of both income and ethnicity. The disparities in life expectancy across some groups are large. When groups are broken into detailed categories by race, gender, and geographical area, the gap between the highest and lowest life expectancies at birth for race-county combinations in the United States is more than 35 years (Murray et al. 2006). Furthermore, differences in life expectancy across demographic groups have increased in recent decades (Freedman et al. 2004).[1] For example, disparity in life expectancy between whites and blacks is growing. (See Chapter 2.)

Having important distributional (and thus social and political) consequences, the increase in longevity for older persons has occurred mostly among those in the top half of the earnings distribution. A male in the top half of the earnings distribution who reached age 60 in 1972 could expect to live 1.2 years longer than one in the bottom half. By 2001, the gap for 60-year-olds had grown to 5.8 years (Waldron 2007). This large difference has major implications for public policy dealing with the effects of longer life expectancy.

It is also important to note, however, that life expectancy improved for both earnings groups. Measuring life expectancy from birth for the male cohort born in 1912, researchers found that, among those in the bottom half of the earnings distribution, 50 percent were still alive at age 77. Those in the top half of the earnings distribution reached age 79 before their survival rate fell to 50 percent. By comparison, for the male cohort born in 1941, the ages at which mortality reached 50 percent improved to 80 and 86, respectively. Thus, this measure of life expectancy lengthened by three years for males in the bottom half and by seven years for those in the top half.

The policy debate over the equity effects of raising the early retirement age for Social Security or other changes based on improvements in life expectancy is determined to a large extent by the choice of the baseline comparison. Often in policy issues relating to equity, the choice of the baseline comparison is key. If the baseline comparison is the present, then the differences in life expectancy by income are key. If the baseline comparison is the past, then the improvement in life expectancy by all groups is important. In that case, the increase in life expectancy for all groups can be viewed as justifying raising the early retirement age, which would leave no group worse off compared to the past. That is the perspective taken in this book.

## Other Demographic Changes

As well as changes in life expectancy, changes in retirement age and in the age at which people enter the labor force also affect Social Security and pension financing. In 1940, when Social Security first paid retirement benefits and when the earliest age at which those benefits could be collected was 65, workers reaching age 65 lived, on average, for another 13 years. Many workers began work at age 18, immediately after high school. These workers could work for as long as 47 years before reaching the normal retirement age of 65. For a full-career worker, a pension plan could anticipate the amount of contributions needed to finance 13 years in retirement and could make these contributions over a 47-year period. The number of years a full-career worker spent in retirement was thus between one-fourth and one-third of the number of years that worker had spent in the labor force.

Now most workers claim Social Security retirement benefits at age 62 rather than at age 65. Many entered the labor force at a later age than in the past, often at age 21 or even older, rather than at age 18. This leaves about 40 years of work possible before an expected retirement at age 62, with a remaining life expectancy of approximately 20 years. Thus, a pension plan can anticipate about 40 years of contributions for a full-career worker to finance about 20 years of retirement. The number of years spent in retirement is about half of the number of years spent in the labor force, up from less than one-third in 1940 (American Academy of Actuaries 2006). This book considers both changes in retirement age (see, in particular, Chapter 4) and changes in life expectancy.

## The Cost of Increased Longevity

What does increased longevity cost? Projected longevity increases are a major cause of the projected funding shortfalls for Social Security. The Congressional Budget Office (CBO) has estimated the cost savings if benefits were indexed for life expectancy, a proposal considered in this book. With that change, increases in life expectancy would reduce annual benefits received by future retirees. That one change would eliminate 43 percent of Social Security's long-term deficit (CBO 2005).

In the long term, increases in longevity are the main aspect of demographic change that increases Social Security's costs. A study by the Social Security Administration indicates that if a baseline of 2008 is chosen, increases in life expectancy after that date have little effect on program costs through changes in the dependency ratio for the first 20 years, but after 2030 they are projected to account for all the changes in the dependency ratio (Goss 2010). The dependency ratio is a key parameter in determining the costs of providing Social Security benefits. Thus, in the long term, increases in life expectancy are key.

A related issue to increasing life expectancy is population aging. Populations age when people live longer and when fertility decreases, which results in there being fewer young people in the population. The aging of the baby boom population bulge also contributes to population aging. This book focuses specifically on increased life expectancy in terms of its effects and the possible policy responses, and only deals with population aging and the population bulge peripherally.

While the future course of life expectancy is unknown, the Social Security Administration, other government agencies, and most demographers predict that it will continue to increase. One reason to expect that life expectancy at older ages will continue increasing is that the United States lags behind a number of countries in this regard. In 2005, life expectancies at age 65 for women and for men in this country were 19.0 and 17.0 years. In that year, the figures in France were 19.8 and 18.2. In Japan, they were 23.4 and 18.5. Compared to U.S. figures, the figures were higher for women in at least 17 countries and were higher for men in at least 13 countries (National Center for Health Statistics 2009a).

## THIS BOOK

The remainder of the book is organized into four parts, the first three of which all discuss various policy responses to increased longevity. The first of these, Part 1, deals with issues relating to the labor market for older workers. It considers changes in the health of older workers and changes in job requirements by employers, two issues affecting whether older workers could work longer. It argues that the evidence supports the ability of most people to extend their working lives, making feasible a policy that would encourage later retirement. The widespread strikes in France when this was proposed in 2010 indicate that this can be an unpopular proposal.

Part 2 of the book considers how Social Security policy is affected by increasing life expectancy. Its first chapter examines automatic adjustment mechanisms that could be adopted to restore and maintain Social Security solvency, including raising the early retirement age. Social Security currently adjusts benefits for postponed benefit receipt so that, for a person with average actuarial life expectancy, the present expected value of benefits is roughly equal at age 62 or 63, thus providing neither an incentive nor a disincentive to postpone retirement. For people expecting to live longer than the actuarial average, there is an incentive to postpone retirement.[2]

The question could be asked, "Why raise the Social Security early retirement age, given that Social Security provides incentives for some workers to postpone retirement already?" Social Security provides incentives for workers with longer-than-average life expectancy to postpone retirement because the increased benefits they receive are for more than the average number of years. However, the actuarial adjustment for postponed receipt of benefits is insufficient to provide such incentives to people with shorter-than-average life expectancy. In any case, regardless of the incentives, many people are shortsighted and take benefits at age 62, the earliest age at which benefits are available, even though they would be better off financially if they postponed benefit receipt.

In discussions about policy reform of Social Security, participants often find the issue of raising the retirement age confusing. Often, when those discussions refer to the Social Security retirement age, they are referring to the normal retirement age, which is a technical term for the age at which a person can receive what are considered to be full benefits. For people currently aged 62, that age is 66, but changes already enacted into law raise it to age 67 for people born in 1960 and later. When this book refers to raising the retirement age for Social Security, it is referring to the early retirement age, which is 62, but which for more than 20 years at the start of Social Security was 65. The reason the issue of raising the retirement age can be misleading is that raising the normal retirement age would have no effect on the earliest age at which people can receive Social Security benefits, which continues to be 62. It is equivalent, instead, to a benefit cut.

Retirement income policy is fundamentally about making hard choices. This holds true for both individuals and national policymakers. An alternative to workers working longer is to increase workers' savings and worker and employer contributions to Social Security and pension funds to pay for retirements that are being lengthened by increasing life expectancy. Whatever changes are made in public policy, that option with respect to personal savings remains for individuals: those who wish to retire early can plan to do so by raising their savings. That said, many individuals find retirement planning, with its long time frame, difficult to do.

In the public arena, politicians and the general public face the possible choice, among others, between raising the Social Security payroll tax and raising the Social Security early retirement age, so that benefits currently receivable at age 62 would instead be received at age 63. Any change in the early retirement age would presumably take effect many years in the future, with a phase-in period starting at that point. Given the widespread antipathy toward raising Social Security contributions, and the improvements in the ability of people to work in their early sixties, this book presents the case for raising the early retirement age.

The section on Social Security also contains a proposal for a new benefit, called longevity insurance, that would be payable starting at age 82. It focuses on two vulnerable groups: first, workers who retire at age 62 in poor health, with poor work prospects and little in retirement resources other than Social Security; and second, retirees in their eighties who have spent down their non–Social Security assets and rely primarily on Social Security benefits.

Part 3 of the book looks at private pension policy as it is affected by increasing life expectancy. It discusses issues for 401(k) plans and for defined benefit plans. The most common type of pension plan in the United States is the 401(k) plan, named after the section of the tax code that enabled it. It is a defined contribution plan, where the worker's benefit is based on the amount accumulated in a pension account. Ways to encourage more people to annuitize their 401(k) plan account balances are discussed.

The chapter on defined benefit plans proposes a new type of defined benefit plan, called a life expectancy–indexed defined benefit plan.

Defined benefit plans are traditional pension plans, where the worker's benefit at retirement is typically based on a benefit formula that incorporates years of work and some measure of the worker's salary. A life expectancy–indexed defined benefit plan would incorporate a feature of defined contribution plans that provide annuities. It would "de-risk" defined benefit plans of most of the longevity risk that plan sponsors bear currently, which could encourage employers to provide defined benefit plans.

The book's fourth and final part is its conclusion, which consists of a chapter on policy recommendations. Yet public policy books shouldn't be read like novels: readers need not wait for the suspense to be resolved at the end. While this book first presents the evidence concerning the ability of many people to extend their working lives and the evidence concerning other policy prescriptions, readers who care more about the policy prescriptions and less about the development of the material supporting them should read the last chapter first. The next several pages provide a brief overview of some of the major policy recommendations.

## FIVE POLICY RECOMMENDATIONS

While the final chapter provides a more detailed summary and justification of the policy recommendations I make, this section provides an overview of five of the major recommendations (Table 1.1). Three of the recommendations involve Social Security. While changes concerning Social Security that involve retrenchment are not popular, these changes are recommended within the context of recognizing that some changes are needed to restore solvency.

### 1) Index Social Security Benefits for Life Expectancy

First, I recommend that Social Security benefits be indexed for life expectancy, so that increases in life expectancy would not cause an increase in the lifetime value of pension benefits. This type of indexation has been adopted by Sweden for its social security program.[3] From a lifetime perspective, this change is not a benefit cut, but it does result in lower annual benefits than otherwise.

**Table 1.1  Overview of Major Policy Recommendations**

| Policy area | Policy | Goal |
| --- | --- | --- |
| 1) Social Security | Life-expectancy indexing of benefits | Help restore solvency |
| 2) Social Security | Raise early retirement age from 62 to 63 | Raise benefit level to offset benefit cuts |
| 3) Social Security | Longevity insurance benefit payable at age 82 | Provide better targeting of benefits; offset benefit cuts |
| 4) 401(k) plans | Require that annuities be offered when a defined benefit plan is not also offered | Encourage annuitization of 401(k) plans |
| 5) Defined benefit plans | Life expectancy–indexed DB plan | Encourage provision of defined benefit plans |

SOURCE: Author's recommendations.

With this type of indexation, every year, for each new retirement cohort, benefits would be slightly adjusted downward to take into account the effect of increased life expectancy on the lifetime value of benefits. The adjustment would occur for each cohort only once; thus, benefits received at retirement would face no further adjustments for continued increases in life expectancy during the retirement period.

According to calculations done by the CBO (2005), this change would reduce the present value of the 75-year Social Security deficit by 0.5 percent of payroll, a reduction in the present value of the deficit, in the CBO's calculations, of 42 percent. The Congressional Budget Office estimates that with this change the date of Social Security insolvency would be 2059, which is sufficiently far into the future that no further cost-saving changes would need to be made for at least a decade. This type of indexation results in a reduced replacement rate over time, an issue addressed by the following proposal.

## 2) Raise the Early Retirement Age

Second, I recommend that, using a long delay and phase-in period, the Social Security early retirement age be raised from 62 to 63. This change is consistent with policy in Germany, the United Kingdom, Switzerland, and a number of other countries that have early retirement ages of 63 or higher (Turner 2007). An early retirement age of 63 is two years younger than what the early retirement age for Social Security was when President Franklin Roosevelt signed the Social Security Act and benefits were first paid in 1940. Life expectancy has increased for all demographic groups since 1940.

This change could be accomplished in one of two ways. First, it could be done so that persons retiring at age 63 would receive the advantage of the actuarial adjustment currently provided for postponing benefit receipt from age 62 to 63. This approach would raise the level of benefits for persons who previously would have retired at age 62, by providing an additional boost in their benefits if they worked the extra year. This approach would not affect Social Security's long-run finances. Alternatively, the second approach would provide, at age 63, benefits currently receivable at age 62. That approach does not cut annual benefits for those who were going to retire at age 62, but it does cut lifetime benefits and would result in cost savings.

### 3) Add a Longevity Insurance Benefit

My third recommendation for Social Security is to add a new type of benefit called a longevity insurance benefit. Longevity insurance would be a type of social insurance providing benefits to qualifying persons at an advanced age—initially set at age 82, but automatically increased to take into account future increases in life expectancy.

As retirees age, they face an increased risk of poverty as they spend down their non–Social Security assets. A longevity insurance benefit would be paid by Social Security starting at age 82 for people who had at least 20 years of covered earnings and were receiving Social Security benefits below a fixed level. Payment would not require an application or a means test; it would occur automatically. It would be a targeted, cost-effective way of addressing poverty at advanced old age. Longevity insurance could be included in a reform package to restore Social Security solvency that contained benefit cuts, so that it would prevent benefit cuts from increasing poverty rates at advanced older ages. It would not have the problem of low take-up rate, which Supplemental Security Income (SSI) has, because eligible retirees would automatically receive it.

## 4) Require 401(k) Plans to Offer Annuities, if They Are the Sole Plans

A fourth recommendation I make is to require that 401(k) plans offer annuities when those plans are provided by an employer that does not also provide a defined benefit plan meeting minimum standards of generosity. Initially, most 401(k) plans were supplemental plans provided by employers who also provided defined benefit plans. That is no longer the case, but they still are regulated to a large extent as if they were supplemental plans. This requirement would treat 401(k) plans that are the primary plan as pension plans rather than as savings plans, as they are currently treated.

## 5) Permit Life Expectancy–Indexed Defined Benefit Plans

Because of the different types of risks that defined benefit and defined contribution plans impose on participants, a pension system would be more diversified if it provided both defined benefit and defined contribution plans to most workers. In order to encourage employer provision of defined benefit plans, my fifth recommendation is that pension law be amended to permit a new type of defined benefit (DB) plan, called a life expectancy–indexed DB plan. This plan would allow more efficient bearing of life expectancy risk than is currently permitted in defined benefit plans, which may encourage employers to provide such a plan.

With a life expectancy–indexed DB plan, at retirement the generosity of the plan would be adjusted to take into account improvements in life expectancy, which would be analogous to annuitizing a defined contribution plan account using current life expectancy, or to the changes proposed for Social Security. Thus, cohort life expectancy risk would be shifted to workers, who can bear it more easily than plan sponsors because the workers are the prime beneficiaries of the increase in life expectancy. This recommendation for defined benefit plans is equivalent to Recommendation 1 for Social Security.

## CONCLUSIONS

The premise of the book is that public policy should recognize longevity policy as a distinct policy area. Policy should be developed that is directly related to the effects of increasing life expectancy. Rather than separately treating the issues raised by life expectancy concerning Social Security, pensions, and work at older ages, a unified approach should be developed that recognizes their interrelationship. A unified approach may facilitate the needed changes in each of the areas. Dealing with only one area may be more difficult and less effective than dealing with all the areas at the same time. Together, the policies recommended in this book would encourage work at older ages, move Social Security toward solvency, provide better targeting of Social Security benefits, increase annuitization of 401(k) accounts, and encourage employers to provide defined benefit plans.

## Notes

1. Healthy life expectancy, which combines morbidity and mortality, is an indicator of expected years of life lived in full health without disease or disability.
2. Actuarial life expectancy is based solely on a person's age, and sometimes gender. Some people have family histories where they expect to live substantially longer than their actuarial life expectancy.
3. In this book, I follow the practice of uppercasing "Social Security" when referring to the U.S. system, and of lowercasing the term when referring to social security systems in other countries or to social security systems generally.

# Part 1

# Labor Market Policy
# toward Older Workers

# 2

# Can Older Workers Extend Their Work Lives?

## Changes in Health and Job Requirements

This chapter addresses the question of whether workers would be able to work longer without undue hardship. This issue is key in formulating policies to deal with the improvements in longevity. Specifically, this chapter focuses on working past age 62, the early retirement age for Social Security. The question of whether it would be feasible for more workers to work longer has two parts. First, have older workers' capabilities changed over the past several decades in ways that would facilitate their continued employment? Second, have job requirements changed in ways that would facilitate continued employment for older workers?

While worker capabilities and job requirements can be viewed separately, ultimately the matching of job requirements and worker capabilities is what matters. Thus, the ultimate questions are "What percentage of the older workforce cannot find jobs that match their capabilities as they age?" and "How has that percentage changed over recent decades?"

In examining changes in worker capabilities and job requirements, this chapter looks back over the past 20 to 40 years, depending on availability of data, and focuses on people in their late fifties and their sixties.

## WHY WORK LONGER?

In a wealthy country such as the United States, some people question why the issue of extending work lives is even discussed. As society grows wealthier, people want to spend more of their wealth on leisure, including longer periods of retirement. Can't we as a society afford an ever-increasing share of adult life spent in retirement?

15

Paying for retirement is expensive. Longer retirements mean greater costs for social programs. It also means workers need greater savings, which means reduced consumption while working. Workers individually and society generally need to face the hard choice of saving more to fund longer retirements or taking steps to postpone retirement. While saving more is an option to postponing retirement, the reality is that many workers are not setting aside sufficient savings to fund longer retirement. One study of retirement savings has found that roughly half of households have insufficient retirement savings, and the shortfall is staggering. The total shortfall in 2010 was $6.6 trillion dollars, a shortfall roughly equal to the amount of savings in retirement plans (Retirement USA 2010).

In this era of increasing longevity and insufficient savings, older workers able to do so may gain a number of advantages from working longer. They have more years to save and fewer years to spend during retirement. They have more years to earn benefit credits in traditional defined benefit plans and Social Security, and more years to accumulate assets in defined contribution plans. Benefits that are paid as annuities will start at a later date, and early retirement reductions will be smaller. They face less concern about inflation eroding the real value of their benefits during a lengthy period of retirement.

In addition to these savings and cost issues favoring longer work lives, aspects of the labor market are more favorable to working longer than in the past. Many people have jobs that are less physically strenuous than in the past. The move from defined benefit plans to defined contribution plans reduces pension disincentives to continue to work at older ages. Changes in Social Security have raised the incentives to continue working past age 62, up to age 70.

Yet working longer is not advantageous for all older workers. For example, older workers with relatively short life expectancy reduce their expected lifetime Social Security benefits by postponing receipt of benefits. This contrasts with older workers who have relatively long life expectancy, who raise their expected lifetime benefits because of the increase in annual benefits that comes from postponing retirement, and because of the relatively long period over which they will receive the increased benefits.

Statistics show that some men are working longer than did their counterparts in the recent past. Starting in the 1990s, the decades-long decline or stagnation of labor force participation of men age 65 and older was reversed, and the labor force participation rate for men in that age group began to increase (Maestas and Zissimopoulos 2010). In 1995, 51 percent of males aged 62 were working (Quinn 1999), but by 2005, that figure had risen to 60 percent (Burkhauser and Rovba 2009).

This chapter examines how changes in worker capabilities and job requirements over the past few decades affect the ability of older workers to work past the Social Security early retirement age of 62. This issue arises because a possible reform of Social Security would raise the early retirement age from 62 to 63. This change might be made in conjunction with raising the normal retirement age in order to offset the reduction in annual benefits that workers would receive when retiring at the early retirement age. The normal retirement age, also called the full retirement age, is the age set in the Social Security benefit formula where there is no reduction for early retirement. The name can be misleading—it does not refer to when people actually (normally) retire. The normal retirement age is currently 66 but is scheduled to increase to 66½ for people who will reach age 62 in 2017, and to 67 for people who will reach age 62 in 2022.

## HEALTH INDICATORS AFFECTING THE ABILITY TO WORK AT OLDER AGES

A survey in the 1980s concluded that persons aged 62–67 had experienced increased longevity over the previous 20 years but that their health had worsened on average. Their health on average had declined because advances in medicine were enabling more unhealthy people to live to older ages. Disability rates and morbidity rates had increased (Chapman, LaPlante, and Wilensky 1986). While recognizing that improvements in medical technology and in healthy behaviors could reverse this trend, the study projected that the trend of worsening health at older ages would continue, because of improvements in medical care that enable unhealthy people to live longer than in the past. After looking at trends in life expectancy, this section assesses the accuracy of the predictions of that study and shows that its gloomy assessment was incorrect.

## Life Expectancy

Improvements in life expectancy, if accompanied by better health, allow workers to extend their work life and still enjoy a longer retirement. While life expectancy has improved generally in the United States, its rate of improvement has differed across demographic groups.

### Population life expectancy by age

Improvements in life expectancy can be measured different ways. Life expectancy at age 65 rose from 14.4 years in 1960 to 18.4 years in 2000, an increase of four years (Robinson 2007). Let's make a slightly different comparison: a person aged 62 in 1960 had a life expectancy of 14.6 years, which was the life expectancy of someone aged 67 in 2000. Thus, by this measure there has been an improvement of five years. A third way to measure changes in life expectancy is to compare the age in 2000 at which workers would have the same risk of death as a worker aged 62 in 1960. The average person aged 68 in 2000 had the same risk of death over the following two years as the average person aged 62 in 1960, an improvement of six years over four decades (Cutler, Liebman, and Smyth 2006).

### Gender and race differences in life expectancy

Examining differences over the past four decades in life expectancy by gender, a man aged 65 had a life expectancy of 12.8 years in 1960, compared to 16.8 years in 2003. The comparable figures for women are 15.8 years and 19.8 years (Robinson 2007). Thus, for both men and women life expectancy over this period increased by four years, or about one year per decade.

Life expectancy improvements for blacks have lagged behind those for whites. Life expectancy at age 65 was similar for black and white males in 1950 and 1960 and for many years following. In 1975, black and white males at age 65 both had a life expectancy of 13.7 years (Table 2.1). However, by 2003, black male life expectancy was 14.9 years, while that of white males was 16.9 years (CDC 2003b). Thus, life expectancy had improved for both groups, but had improved more for whites than for blacks, by two full years. While the reasons no doubt are complex, differential changes in smoking and in obesity may be factors.

**Table 2.1  Life Expectancy at Age 65, 1950–2005 (by number of years)**

| Year | White men | White women | Black men | Black women |
|------|-----------|-------------|-----------|-------------|
| 1950 | 12.8 | 15.1 | 12.9 | 14.9 |
| 1960 | 12.9 | 15.9 | 12.7 | 15.1 |
| 1975 | 13.7 | 18.1 | 13.7 | 17.5 |
| 2006 | 17.1 | 19.8 | 15.1 | 18.6 |

SOURCE: National Center for Health Statistics (2009b).

Policy analysts sometimes argue that raising the early retirement age in Social Security would hurt blacks more than whites because blacks have a shorter life expectancy than whites. Instead of making comparisons across racial groups, however, we can make an intergenerational comparison between blacks currently and blacks in the early 1960s. In that case, the early retirement age could be raised by at least a year. Doing so would still result in a higher number of years in retirement for blacks and the same percentage of adult life spent in retirement in comparison to that experienced by the black cohort retiring in the early 1960s.

If we take a more granular approach, life expectancy by race can be further divided into racial differences by geographic location. Doing so produces much greater differences in life expectancy than the differences just discussed (Murray et al. 2006). The gap in life expectancy at birth between the 3.4 million high-risk urban black males and the 5.6 million Asian females was 20.7 years in 2001. The gap in life expectancy at birth between the highest and lowest race-county categories (i.e., race average at the county level) was more than 33 years. The life expectancy at birth for Native American males in certain counties in South Dakota was 58 years, which fell 33 years short of the life expectancy for Asian females in Bergen County, New Jersey, of 91 years.

For some narrowly defined groups, life expectancy at birth actually worsened between 1982 and 2001. For example, life expectancy worsened for low-income females in Appalachia and the Mississippi Valley over that period. These disparities, which are enormous by international standards, complicate efforts at structuring public policy to deal with improvements in life expectancy, and suggest that policy changes need to take into account the situation of vulnerable groups. It is not possible to raise the early retirement age for Social Security and keep every race-geographical location group as well off as its comparison group for an earlier period. However, for major demographic groups, it is possible to meet that criterion.

## Socioeconomic differences in life expectancy

Studies have documented differences in mortality by income, education, and marital status (Brown 2001). Mirroring differences by race, improvements in life expectancy have not occurred at the same pace for all socioeconomic groups. In particular, the historical advantage in life expectancy of higher education groups compared to lower education groups has expanded over the past four decades for men but decreased for women. In 1960, the mortality rates for white men aged 65 to 70 at the top of the education distribution were 10 percent lower than for those at the bottom. Mortality rates have decreased for both the upper and lower education groups. However, the improvements were much more rapid for upper education groups—mortality rates were 70 percent lower for the upper income and education groups in the 1990s compared to the lower income and education groups (Diamond and Orszag 2004).

## Health

As we have just discussed, people generally are living longer. However, those alive at the ages at which increased work might occur may be less healthy on average than in the past because medical improvements are allowing more unhealthy people to survive to older ages. This effect of increased life expectancy on health at older ages was debated during the early 1980s when the 1983 Social Security Amendments were passed, raising the normal retirement age. At that time it appeared that health at older ages was declining (Social Security Administration 1986).

Many jobs have low physical requirements, so robust health is not required to perform them. Thus, the low end of health may be more relevant currently than the upper end for determining ability to work for most jobs. Since the early 1980s, the percentage of older persons reporting that they are in fair or poor health has decreased (Table 2.2). Between 1982 and 2005, for the population aged 50–64, all demographic groups examined showed a decline in the percentage of persons reporting themselves in fair or poor health. For example, for blacks that percentage declined from 41 to 26 percent (Robinson 2007).

**Table 2.2  Self-Reported Health Status Rated as Fair or Poor, Aged 50–64, by Gender, Race, and Ethnicity, 1982–2005, Selected Years (%)**

| Year | Women | Men | Non-Hispanic blacks | Hispanics | Non-Hispanic whites |
|---|---|---|---|---|---|
| 1982 | 24.4 | 23.2 | 40.9 | 29.6 | 21.7 |
| 1985 | 21.0 | 20.4 | 37.1 | 25.3 | 18.6 |
| 1990 | 18.1 | 18.0 | 31.8 | 24.2 | 15.9 |
| 1995 | 20.2 | 18.5 | 33.2 | 28.6 | 16.7 |
| 2000 | 16.4 | 15.4 | 26.9 | 23.9 | 13.6 |
| 2005 | 16.3 | 15.8 | 26.4 | 25.2 | 13.9 |
| Difference, 1982–2005 | 8.1 | 7.4 | 14.5 | 4.4 | 7.8 |

SOURCE: Robinson (2007).

The percentage of both men and women reporting their health as fair or poor has also declined. This trend suggests that a growing proportion of the older population would be capable of working. In the mid-1970s, 29 percent of men aged 62 reported their health as fair or poor. Two decades later, in the mid-1990s, that percentage was not reached by men reporting their health until they hit their early seventies—an improvement of 10 years over a 20-year period (Cutler, Liebman, and Smyth 2006). The improvement in self-reported health was more rapid than the increase in life expectancy.

While the prevalence of self-reported fair or poor health declined for both men and women, a more complex pattern emerges for other demographic groups (Table 2.2). The largest decline over the period 1982–2005 for people aged 50–64 self-reporting fair or poor health occurred for non-Hispanic blacks, causing a move toward convergence for blacks and whites. However, Hispanics have seen basically no improvement by this measure over the past 20 years.

Despite these general trends of improvement over the past several decades, more-recent evidence is mixed concerning trends in health, and therefore the ability to work. Some evidence suggests a reversal in the trend of improving health at older ages (Korczyk 2002). A study of baby boomers aged 51–56 concludes that their self-reported health was worse than that of people the same age 12 years earlier (Soldo et al. 2006). Possible explanations for that finding include that obesity has increased, that baby boomers are more likely than earlier generations to complain about health issues, that improvements in diagnosis and in pharmaceutical treatments have made people more aware of their health problems, or that this trend is the result of increased stress. The percentage of the population aged 50–64 reporting their health as excellent or very good has increased over the past several decades (Robinson 2007). However, the incidence of diabetes among the population aged 55–60 rose between 1992 and 2002 (Johnson 2004). Other evidence indicates that the prevalence of diabetes has declined among non-Hispanic whites aged 50–64, while it has increased among non-Hispanic blacks that age (Robinson 2007). Thus, the recent evidence is mixed, and cannot be simply summarized as a trend of overall improvements.

## Disability

Disability rates for people in their fifties, sixties, and older have declined over the past two decades. National Long-Term Care Survey (NLTCS) data indicate that the incidence of chronic disability (lasting at least three months) declined for the population aged 65–74 for the years from 1984 to 1999 (Spillman 2003). Estimates from several national sources show that the proportion of the noninstitutionalized population aged 70 and older with severe disabilities has declined since the mid-1990s (Freedman et al. 2004). Functional limitations among men aged 60 to 74 have also declined over time (Costa 2002).

Reasons for the decline in disability incidence include improved medical technology and health care, better personal health practices, better technical aids helping people with disabilities, reduced exposure to infectious diseases, and increased education and living standards (Korczyk 2002). One study found that improvements in medical care relating to cardiovascular disease led to a significant part of the decline in disability among adults (Cutler, Liebman, and Smyth 2006). Surveying a number of measures of health status, including disability rates, the same study has concluded that people aged 62 in the 1960s and 1970s were equivalent to people in their early seventies today, an improvement of about a decade.

The future is not as clear as the past concerning these issues. Similar to the finding of mixed recent evidence concerning health trends, some evidence suggests that the decline in disability rates may have stopped or reversed. Comparing people aged 55–61 in 2004 with people of the same age range in 1992, researchers found that the reported incidence of work limitations was 19 percent for the 2004 group, versus 18 percent for the earlier group, a difference that is not statistically significant (Mermin, Johnson, and Murphy 2006).

A survey of a number of studies of disability at older ages (Freedman, Martin, and Schoeni 2002) has concluded that disability rates declined at older ages over the decade from the late 1980s to the late 1990s. However, disability rates at younger ages have been increasing. Between 1990 and 1996, disabilities among those in their forties increased slightly, perhaps because of the increased incidence of obesity (Lakdawalla, Bhattacharya, and Goldman 2004).

In sum, life expectancy at older ages has increased for all major demographic groups. Compared to the 1980s, disability rates have declined and self-reported health has improved for persons at older ages. These patterns also hold for demographic groups viewed as vulnerable because of their higher old-age poverty rates—blacks and women. However, over the past 10 or 15 years, mixed evidence suggests that improvements in health and disability rates may have slowed or, for some groups, possibly reversed.

## FACTORS AFFECTING HEALTH AT OLDER AGES

While the advance of medicine influences the health of people at older working ages, behavioral factors also affect older persons' ability to continue working. To better understand the trends in health and ability to work at older ages, this section examines some of the underlying determinants.

### Increased Education

Higher education levels are associated with better health, presumably in part because better-educated people are better informed about healthy lifestyles. They also tend to have higher income, better access to medical care, and possibly better diets. The percentage of the older population with at least four years of high school education has increased (Table 2.3).

Workers with higher levels of education are more likely to continue working at older ages. One study found that the increase in college graduation rates combined with a decline in high school dropout rates accounted for about a third of the increase in workers' expectations that they would work past age 62 (Mermin, Johnson, and Murphy 2006).

Education level plays an important role in the downward trend in disability rates over the past 20 years. That trend appears to have occurred only among persons who completed high school (Schoeni, Freedman, and Wallace 2001). Disability rates have not improved among people who have not completed high school, and who are thus more likely to have physically demanding jobs.

## Decline in Smoking

Smoking is a major health risk factor. The percentage of adults who smoke has declined since 1960: in that year, more than 50 percent of men and 30 percent of women smoked. By comparison, in 2004, 23 percent of men and 19 percent of women smoked.

Smoking is closely linked to having a low level of education and thus to working in occupations that are physically demanding. In 2004,

**Table 2.3  Percentage of Population with Educational Attainment of Four Years of High School or More, Aged 55–64, by Race and Ethnicity, 1960–2004, Selected Years (%)**

| Year | Blacks | Hispanics | Whites |
|------|--------|-----------|--------|
| 1960 | 10.1 | — | 28.4 |
| 1970 | 16.2 | 22.4 | 42.7 |
| 1980 | 30.2 | 29.0 | 63.8 |
| 1990 | 46.4 | 40.0 | 73.2 |
| 2000 | 67.8 | 47.2 | 83.6 |
| 2004 | 76.4 | 56.5 | 87.7 |
| Difference, 1960–2004 | 66.3 | — | 59.3 |

NOTE: — = data not available.
SOURCE: Robinson (2007).

adults without a high school degree were three times as likely to smoke as persons with a bachelor's degree or higher (National Center for Health Statistics 2006).

The percentage of the population aged 55–64 currently smoking declined over the period 1965–2004 for both blacks and whites. The decline was less for blacks than whites, but the rates for the two groups converged, as blacks started from a lower level (Table 2.4).

**Increase in Obesity**

Increases over the past few decades in the rate of obesity may have a negative effect on the health of the older working-age population. Since 1960, the proportion of adults who are overweight but not obese has remained steady at about one-third. However, the percentage who are obese has roughly doubled since the late 1970s (National Center for Health Statistics 2006). Two-thirds of adult Americans are overweight, including one-third who are obese. Obesity rates for both blacks and whites have increased (Table 2.5).

Obesity is associated with adult-onset diabetes (CDC 2003a). It is also linked to hypertension, high cholesterol, heart disease, and some forms of cancer. The earlier the onset of obesity, the more serious its health effects may be. However, people who exercise regularly and are both fat and fit may suffer fewer consequences of being overweight. Researchers hold differing views about the severity of the effects of the obesity epidemic on disability, particularly when obesity begins in childhood (Olshansky et al. 2005; Preston 2005).

**Table 2.4 Percentage of Population Smoking Cigarettes, Aged 55–64, by Race, 1965–2004, Selected Years (%)**

| Year | Black | White |
|------|-------|-------|
| 1965 | 31.0 | 36.4 |
| 1974 | 38.7 | 33.4 |
| 1983–1985 | 35.8 | 29.0 |
| 1990–1991 | 24.9 | 23.2 |
| 2000–2001 | 25.9 | 21.6 |
| 2002–2004 | 24.8 | 20.0 |
| Difference, 1965–2004 | −6.2 | −16.4 |

SOURCE: Robinson (2007).

**Table 2.5  Obesity Rates for Males, by Race and Ethnicity, 2000–2008 (%)**

| Year | Non-Hispanic white | Non-Hispanic black | Mexican American |
|---|---|---|---|
| 1999–2000 | 34.3 | 26.4 | 29.7 |
| 2007–2008 | 38.4 | 38.0 | 35.8 |

SOURCE: Flegal et al. (2010).

The effect of obesity on increased mortality rates may, however, have decreased over the past several decades, perhaps from improvements in pharmaceuticals (Fiebelkorn 2006). Some of the effects of obesity—high blood pressure, high cholesterol, and diabetes—can be controlled pharmacologically. However, because of the large population without health insurance currently—some 50 million Americans—the ability to offset the health effects of obesity is not available to many. Thus, obesity may have a more limited effect on health for people with adequate medical care than for lower-income persons lacking good medical care. If health care reform, passed by Congress in 2010, succeeds in extending health insurance to uncovered populations, this difference in effect would be reduced. However, while obesity has not led to declines overall in life expectancy, the increase in obesity among people in their sixties and older in the United States may explain why the improvements in longevity at older ages have been less rapid in the United States than in other advanced countries.

## ABILITY TO WORK AT OLDER AGES

This section examines direct measures of the ability of people to work in their late fifties and early-to-mid-sixties. The ability to work at older ages clearly varies across job types that have differing physical requirements. However, the desire to work at older ages also varies across jobs. For example, in the University of California statewide system, the average age for retirement of professors is 66, but the average age for retirement of staff, who are in the same pension plan, is 60 (University of California 2010). This difference has important implications for the distributional effects of policies that change the ages at which benefits can be received.

## Health Impairments and Work

In 2003, about 25 percent of early retirees in the age range 62–64 were unable to work because of health impairments (Leonesio, Vaughan, and Wixon 2003). By comparison, in the mid-1980s, 16 percent of new Social Security beneficiaries reported they were unable to work at all, and 17 percent reported they were limited in their ability to work (Social Security Administration 1986).

About as many in the 2003 study that reported they were unable to work received early retirement benefits from Social Security as received Social Security Disability benefits or Supplemental Security Income disability benefits (Leonesio, Vaughan, and Wixon 2003). Some disabled people do not qualify for Social Security Disability Insurance benefits because they do not meet the requirement for having worked a sufficient number of years. The Social Security early retirement benefits appear to serve as an important, unofficial disability benefits program for some early retirees, which is a point to be considered if the early retirement age were to be raised.

## Obesity, Diabetes, and Work

An Australian study documents an association between obesity at older ages and a lower probability of being in the labor force (Australian Institute of Health and Welfare 2005). Among people aged 55–64, the obese were 8 percent less likely to be in the labor force and were 20 percent less likely to be employed full time than the nonobese. The obese also had higher absenteeism rates than the nonobese, suggesting an effect of obesity through health issues on ability to work. A U.S. study has found that obese persons tend to be absent from work due to illness substantially more than nonobese persons (Tucker and Friedman 1998). Burton et al. (1998) reported that greater body mass index (BMI—a measure of the amount by which one is overweight or obese) was associated with a higher probability of short-term disability.[1]

Similarly, people with diabetes at older ages are less likely to work than people without diabetes. Among adults aged 45–64, 51 percent of those with diabetes were working, compared to 72 percent of those without diabetes (National Academy on an Aging Society 2000).

Because both obesity and diabetes have increased over the past several decades, these two factors would lead to a decreased ability to work at older ages for some people. However, their effects may have been offset by other changes affecting the ability to work, including changes in the physical demands of jobs.

## THE DECLINE IN PHYSICALLY DEMANDING JOBS

The ability to postpone retirement depends not only on older workers' physical capabilities but also on the physical demands of jobs. Working longer would be facilitated by a decline in the physical demands of jobs.

### Occupations and Industries

Jobs with a high level of physical demands are decreasing in relative number, both because of a decline in the relative number of some types of jobs and because of technological changes that ease the physical requirements of some jobs.

Since the beginning of twentieth century, jobs have shifted from agriculture to manufacturing, and then from manufacturing to the service sector, with the latter shift generally being from physically demanding to less physically demanding jobs. More recently, jobs have shifted to the knowledge economy, where the physical demands are even less. Between 1950 and 2000, the share of jobs in the goods producing sector, which includes manufacturing, mining, and construction, fell from 41 percent to 20 percent (Johnson 2004).

Even within manufacturing, jobs have shifted away from ones with high physical demands. In 1984, 21 percent of those employed in manufacturing industries held a job in a professional, managerial, or technical occupation. By 2000, nearly 28 percent of workers in manufacturing worked in those occupations. Over the period 1984–2000, growth in employment in management, professional, technical, and high-level sales occupational categories accounted for about two-thirds of job growth. Those job categories accounted for only about one-third of jobs at the beginning of the period (Kirsch et al. 2007).

Farm workers were among the occupations with the largest job declines over the period 1988–2000. Technology gains and new labor-saving machinery were the main reasons for the decline, along with increased farm consolidation leading to greater efficiencies. Other physically demanding occupations that experienced a decline in the number of workers included highway maintenance workers (declined 7 percent), butchers and meat cutters (declined 15 percent), fishermen (declined 22 percent), and cannery workers (declined 32 percent) (Alpert and Auyer 2003).

**Direct Measures of Physical Effort**

Jobs can be examined to obtain direct measures of physical effort. While various measures can be used, one measure of physically demanding work is the requirement to lift or carry heavy objects. Between 1950 and 1996, the percentage of the workforce in jobs that required frequent lifting or carrying of objects weighing 25 pounds or more declined from 20 percent to 8 percent (Steuerle, Spiro, and Johnson 1999).

Using a different measure, in 1982, researchers found that 11 percent of older workers reported that their jobs involved heavy strength requirements and 39 percent reported at least medium strength requirements. These measures differed by gender, with 17 percent of men in jobs having heavy strength requirements and 47 percent in jobs having at least medium strength requirements, compared to 4 percent and 29 percent for women (Table 2.6).

Workers whose jobs require physical effort all or most of the time tend to have relatively little education. In 2002, 28 percent of workers aged 55–60 who did not attend college reported that their jobs required physical effort all or most of the time (Johnson 2004).

Between 1992 and 2002, both men and women workers aged 55–60 saw slight declines in the percentage who reported jobs that required substantial physical effort most of the time. The decline was from 20 to 19 percent for men and from 21 to 17 percent for women (Table 2.6). While these figures are not directly comparable to the figures from the early 1980s, they suggest that a substantial decline has occurred since then. However, when disaggregating by education, the decline between

**Table 2.6  Physical Requirements of Jobs, by Gender, 1982–2002, Selected Years (%)**

| Year | Definition of job requirement | Women | Men |
|------|-------------------------------|-------|-----|
| 1982 | Medium or greater strength requirement | 29 | 47 |
| 1992 | Always requires physical effort | 21 | 20 |
| 2002 | Always requires physical effort | 17 | 19 |

NOTE: The data for 1982 are not directly comparable to the later data.
SOURCE: Social Security Administration (1986); Johnson (2004).

1992 and 2002 in percentage of jobs requiring substantial physical effort only occurred for older workers with four or more years of college (Johnson 2004). Thus, the decline did not occur among workers with relatively low education.

## Technology

Technological improvements may lessen the effects of some conditions on ability to work. For example, character recognition software with voice synthesizers allow blind persons to listen to electronic documents being read out loud by a computer, including documents that have been scanned into computers. This technology allows blind persons to function much more independently in a computerized office work environment than in the past. More generally, technology has reduced the physical demands of some jobs, allowing workers to continue working at older ages.

## Stressful Jobs

Although a considerable amount of evidence indicates that the physical demands of work have declined for most workers, some evidence indicates that the stress level of work may have increased. Workers aged 55–60 who reported that their jobs involved a lot of stress increased from 18 to 21 percent between 1992 and 2002 (Johnson 2004). In a survey, three-quarters of workers indicated that they thought jobs had gotten more stressful compared to a generation earlier (NIOSH 1999).

A possible contributing factor to an increase in job stress is the increase in working hours for men. While the average work week varies from year to year, it was 43.0 hours for men in 1969, 1980, and 1990. Since 1990, it has trended upward, and in 2005 it was 45.9. The average work week for women also has varied over time, but without a clear trend.[2]

## Bridge Jobs

Changes in workers' ability to continue working and changes in the prevalence of physically demanding jobs do not tell the whole story. The U.S. labor market is flexible, as are individual workers. Sometimes, workers can adjust to declining physical ability as they age by changing jobs, changing the way they do jobs, or changing the hours they work.

Currently, about half of all workers aged 55–65 are in "bridge jobs," meaning jobs that are a transition from a career job to retirement (Purcell 2002). Bridge jobs can be an adjustment to aging. Bridge jobs sometimes involve different occupations from career jobs. Other types of bridge jobs include self-employed, part-time, and temporary jobs, which provide flexibility to workers who may be unable to continue working full time in their career job because of its physical demands.

Related to bridge jobs, in that it is also a transition to retirement, is phased retirement, which is offered by some employers. With phased retirement, the worker is able to reduce the number of hours worked at his or her career job. While phased retirement seems like a desirable option to allow workers to extend their work lives but not work full time, employers rarely offer it as a formal benefits program because it faces a number of regulatory hurdles (Hill 2010).

## Pensions to Accommodate Early Retirement

Besides changing to less physically demanding jobs at older ages, another option for occupational groups unable to continue working into old age because of the physical demands of their work may be occupational pension plans that permit early retirement (Turner and Guenther 2005). For example, police, firefighters, the military, and miners—

occupations with physically demanding jobs—all have pension plans that permit early retirement.

### Errors in Decision Making

Some people may retire earlier than they otherwise would because of errors in decision making (Hill and Reno 2005). They may overestimate the value of a lump sum benefit from a defined contribution plan in terms of its ability to provide a stream of income during retirement. They may underestimate the effect of inflation eroding the real value of fixed benefits, such as those often provided by defined benefit plans. They may underestimate their life expectancy and overestimate the expected return on their investments (Turner and Witte 2009). As longevity increases, public policy may need to devise ways to help people make better decisions as to when to retire.

In sum, changes have occurred in many workplaces that allow workers to work at older ages. In addition, some workers can change workplaces as they age to find employment that better suits their needs, but some workers retire earlier than would best serve their interests because of errors in decision making.

## PHASED RETIREMENT AND ITS RELEVANCE TO RAISING THE RETIREMENT AGE

Because it is difficult under U.S. pension law for workers to collect a pension while phasing out of work in the same job, people may retire earlier than they want to, doing so in order to access their pension. Currently an employer wishing to offer flexible employment faces numerous barriers arising from the Internal Revenue Code, the Employee Retirement Income Security Act (ERISA), and the Age Discrimination in Employment Act (ADEA) (Penner, Perun, and Steuerle 2007).

Phased retirement can be complex to arrange for employers offering defined benefit plans (Hill 2010). The Pension Protection Act of 2006 permits in-service distributions of defined benefit plan benefits for employees aged 62 or older, which is a step toward facilitating phased retirement at older ages. However, phased retirement starting earlier than age 62 cannot include partial payment of the employee's defined benefit plan benefit. There are also unresolved issues relating to the partial payment of subsidized early retirement benefits because the payment of benefits that are more highly subsidized to younger early retirees may be considered to be age discrimination. Employers would be more likely to encourage phased retirement if this regulatory issue was clarified.

The government could take a proactive stance and provide guidance to employers, who are wary of experimenting under threat of losing their tax deductions for pensions. It could issue guidelines based on the progressive and effective experiments with phased retirement in the public sector.

Phased retirement may allow some older workers to continue working longer than they otherwise would. Some older workers may experience poor health or develop some degree of physical disability that limits their abilities to work full time. Other people may have to provide caregiving services to family members. These concerns may be ameliorated by employment and pension arrangements that allow workers to gradually retire through phasing out of work over a period of time.

Phased retirement may be helpful to older workers in other contexts as well. Some people may need to work in order to supplement their retirement benefits. Others may wish to work for nonfinancial reasons. For these purposes, most people presumably would prefer not to work full time. However, under current employment and pension regulatory conditions, full retirement is generally the only viable choice for those near retirement age who wish to collect their pension. Such an option deprives society of the contributions of these individuals, as it diminishes their opportunity to work. This dilemma could be resolved by arrangements that would allow workers to gradually retire.

Some people prefer retiring from work gradually rather than abruptly. For example, according to the 2001 Retirement Risk Survey, sponsored by the Society of Actuaries, two-thirds of preretirees (66 percent) and almost half of retirees (47 percent) said they were or would have been very or somewhat interested in being able to gradually cut back on the hours they worked at their current job, rather than stopping work all at once when they got closer to retirement. Moreover, almost 2 in 10 retirees (19 percent) described their retirement process as being closest to the following: "gradually reduced the number of hours you worked before stopping completely" (Society of Actuaries 2003).

Some retirees prefer part-time work to full retirement. In a 2003 survey, 70 percent of workers intended to work in retirement and 28 percent of retirees had worked at some time during retirement, according to the Retirement Confidence Survey, conducted by the Employee Benefit Research Institute, Mathew Greenwald and Associates, and the American Savings Education Council (EBRI, ASEC, and Greenwald 2003).

Phased retirement may benefit society. For society, such an arrangement could offset some of the expected labor force shortage, even as it helps contain the costs of pensions. And from a business perspective, it is important to retain and use long-service employees to mentor and train younger workers.

Despite their desirable effects, formal phased retirement arrangements are rare, at least in part because there are a number of barriers to their implementation, including legal barriers, barriers relating to pension plan objectives, and others (Chen and Scott 2003; Penner, Perun, and Steuerle 2002). Though, in principle, hardly anyone opposes phased retirement, it seems workers don't find employers' offers for phased retirement very attractive (Hutchens and Chen 2007). While about 80 percent of older workers work in establishments where employers say that phased retirement is possible, opportunities for phased retirement depend in part on the characteristics of older workers, and are frequently not offered to all workers in an establishment.

## VULNERABLE WORKERS

Generally, people are living longer, are healthier at older ages, and have lower disability rates at older ages than did their counterparts two or more decades ago. The primary criticism, however, to policies that encourage working longer is that doing so places an unfair burden on certain vulnerable groups. These groups fall into three areas: 1) those who have relatively short life expectancies, 2) those who are unable to work at older ages because of physical limitations or the physical demands of their jobs and lack early retirement pensions, and 3) those who become unemployed at older ages and are unable to find other jobs. The research surveyed suggests that workers with low levels of education may be a vulnerable group. Raising the eligibility ages for Social Security may pose problems for workers forced to take early retirement or who are fired or laid off in the few years before the early retirement age because of the greater difficulty older workers have in finding a job. Several studies have attempted to determine the number of people in these vulnerable groups.

In the early 1980s, 19 percent of early retirees were either totally unable to work or had partial limitations and jobs that required heavy physical exertion. If the group of vulnerable workers is expanded to include workers with partial limitations and medium physical requirements of their jobs, plus workers with no physical limitations and heavy physical requirements, the figure would rise to 30 percent of new retirees (Social Security Administration 1986).

One study found that 20 percent of people taking Social Security benefits at age 62 have a health condition that limits the type or amount of work they can do (Panis et al. 2002). That study found that approximately one-half of these early retirees with a health condition did not have a private pension. In addition, approximately one-half of the early retirees with a health condition but without a private pension worked in physically demanding jobs. Approximately 5 percent of all early claimants, or about 2.5 percent of workers, are particularly vulnerable because they have work limitations, do not have a private pension, and work on a physically demanding job. The study did not determine what percentage of these workers would be eligible for Social Security disability benefits.

Another study found that 17 percent of early retirees receiving Social Security benefits have significant impediments to work but would not qualify for Social Security Disability benefits or Supplemental Security Disability benefits (Leonesio, Vaughan, and Wixon 2003). They would not qualify for disability benefits because they would not have worked the minimum required number of years to be eligible for those benefits. They also would not qualify for Supplemental Security Income (SSI) disability benefits because they had assets above the level required by the asset test to qualify.

The self-reported health status of workers whose jobs always required physical effort improved between 1992 and 2002. In 2002,

28 percent of persons aged 55–60 who did not attend college reported that their jobs required physical activity some or most of the time. Of those older workers whose jobs required physical effort all the time, 11 percent in 2002 reported themselves to be in poor health, down from 17 percent in 1992 (Johnson 2004).

People who take Social Security benefits at age 62 frequently have pensions or other resources that would allow them to retire at that age without Social Security, or have jobs where they could continue working. Munnell et al. (2004) find that 4 percent of the population aged 62 are vulnerable, meaning that they have a combination of lack of alternative resources and poor health, which makes it difficult to continue working.

Measuring the extent to which raising the retirement age would hurt vulnerable groups, an earlier study found that less than 10 percent of men who take Social Security benefits at age 62 are both in poor health and have no source of pension income other than Social Security. For women, the figure is 20 percent (Burkhauser, Couch, and Phillips 1996). These findings were later confirmed by a study done by the Congressional Budget Office (1999), which found that if dependency on Social Security retirement benefits at age 62 was defined as resulting from being poor and having a health condition that limited the ability to work, then about 10 percent of the population that age was dependent on those benefits.

In sum, while studies differ to some extent as to precise results, the general conclusion is that a small percentage of the population aged 62, ranging from 2.5 percent to 10 percent, would be unable to continue working and lack sufficient resources to retire, and thus would be vulnerable to hardship resulting from an increase in the early retirement age. The studies, however, have not counted as being vulnerable those older workers who are laid off before age 62, when they become eligible for Social Security, and are unable to find a job and lack a pension. Doing so would increase the percentage of older people who are vulnerable.

## PUBLIC POLICY ISSUES

It may be more difficult to make public policies reflecting improved life expectancy in the United States, with its more racially and ethnically heterogeneous population, than in countries such as Japan, where the population is more homogeneous. Policies that encourage later work in the United States have a differential effect by race because of the racial disparity in life expectancy at older ages.

However, if instead of a cross-sectional approach, the perspective is taken of comparing the ability to work and the physical demands of work currently with the situation for counterparts in the past, the pattern is clear. Both blacks and whites are living longer, people of both races are self-reporting to be healthier at older ages, at least compared to several decades ago, and disability rates at older ages are decreasing.

In Social Security policy, women are often considered to be a vulnerable group because of their higher old-age poverty rates. With respect to longevity policy and raising the early retirement age, however, life expectancy has improved for women (as well as for men) and the percentage of female workers in physically demanding jobs has declined.

One area of uncertainty for future longevity policy concerns the obesity epidemic. The increasing obesity among children is a predictor of increasing obesity among adults. The earlier onset of obesity may lead to more serious health consequences of the condition, which implies that the health effects of obesity that impinge on the ability to work at older ages may be worse in the future than they are currently.

## CONCLUSIONS

This chapter has presented evidence concerning improvements in the ability to work at older ages, and in reductions in the physical demands of many jobs. Based on that evidence, it appears clear that if older workers were economically motivated to do so and the demand for older workers was sufficient, it would be feasible for many older workers to work longer. The age at which one takes retirement is one of the most important financial decisions a worker makes, yet it appears that many workers retire too early, perhaps because of myopia as to the consequences of the decision.

To facilitate a policy favoring postponed retirement, it would be desirable to address barriers to employment at older ages. Many older workers report age discrimination if they are in the situation of looking for a job—for example, if they have been laid off. While this book does not address this issue, it recommends that further research be done on the issue of age discrimination and policies to deal with it. A further topic worth exploring is the issue of educating workers on the benefits of postponing retirement.

## Notes

1. The BMI is calculated by dividing a person's weight (measured in kilograms) by his or her height squared (measured in meters). A BMI of 18.5 to less than 25 is classified as a healthy weight. A BMI of 25 or higher but less than 30 is classified as overweight but not obese. A BMI of 30 or higher is classified as obese.
2. The data in this paragraph came from http://laborsta.ilo.org, an International Labour Office database on labor statistics.

# Part 2

# Social Security Policy

# 3
# Automatic Adjustment Mechanisms to Maintain Social Security's Solvency

The trustees of Social Security project in their 2011 report that Social Security will not have sufficient resources to pay benefits on time starting in 2036.[1] At that point it will be able to pay 75 percent of promised benefits (Social Security Board of Trustees 2011). Over the long term, increases in life expectancy are a major cause of the projected insolvency of Social Security. Yet policies proposed to deal with the projected insolvency often are not directly tied to increases in life expectancy.

In the past, countries have made ad hoc reforms to maintain the solvency of their social security programs. Ad hoc reforms require elected officials to enact legislation each time an adjustment to social security financing is needed. These reforms carry a high degree of political risk for participants because their timing and magnitude are unknown in advance. Their distributional consequences are also unknown in advance, and depend on whether benefits are cut, taxes raised, or both. Because of the political difficulty in legislating cutbacks in social security programs, ad hoc reforms tend to occur in a crisis, with little advance notice to workers and retirees as to the legislated changes (Turner 2007).

Reforms are much easier to enact when benefits are being raised than when they are being cut. In the age of social security retrenchment, some countries have adopted automatic adjustment mechanisms because of the difficulty in enacting unpopular reforms involving benefit cuts. These mechanisms automatically change the social security program depending on economic and demographic developments, such as increases in life expectancy. For example, these policies decide in advance how the social security system will adjust to maintain adequate financing if life expectancy increases. Automatic adjustment mechanisms address the interrelated problems of social security sustainability, the political difficulty for politicians of reforms that involve retrench-

41

ment, and the political risk to workers and retirees associated with ad hoc social security reforms. The automatic adjustments involve benefit cuts, increases in tax revenue, or increases in retirement age.

Automatic adjustment mechanisms can eliminate the need for large program changes made in a crisis. They can eliminate the risk of insufficient financing. They, however, do not eliminate all risk. Workers still face the risk that benefit levels may be reduced, taxes raised, or retirement ages moved back. Risk is reduced in that workers know under what circumstances such changes will occur. Political risk may be reduced with automatic adjustment mechanisms, but it is generally not eliminated, as politicians can always intercede and modify the changes that were designed to be automatic (Turner 2010a).

This chapter surveys high-income countries that have automatic adjustment mechanisms that cut benefits or the accrual of benefits or raise revenue for social security. It describes automatic adjustment mechanisms that achieve and maintain solvency. It concludes by considering how U.S. Social Security could use automatic adjustment mechanisms to improve and maintain solvency.

## THE PROBLEM

The U.S. Social Security program, like most traditional social security programs, is financed on a pay-as-you-go basis, with a relatively small trust fund. The annual inflow of contributions roughly equals the annual outflow of benefits. It historically has maintained a reserve fund to smooth out fluctuations in contributions over the business cycle, and currently it has built up a larger reserve than normal, but that will be drawn down as the baby boom generation retires and receives benefits.

Changes in the ratio of beneficiaries to covered workers (the old-age dependency ratio) play a key role in social security financing in pay-as-you-go systems. The ratio of beneficiaries to covered workers acts like a "price" for benefits, meaning the amount the average worker must pay in social security taxes to raise the average benefit level by one dollar (Turner 1984). For example, when there are 10 workers for every social security beneficiary, a dependency ratio of 0.10, it costs each worker $0.10 to provide one dollar of benefits to each beneficiary.

By contrast, when there are two workers for every beneficiary, a dependency ratio of 0.50, it costs each worker $0.50 to provide one dollar of benefits. Thus, as the dependency ratio rises with an aging population, the "price" to workers of providing social security benefits to retirees on a pay-as-you-go basis also increases. Generally, economics predicts that when the price of something increases, the quantity demanded falls. This occurs because of the law of downward-sloping demand curves. Thus, the increase in the shadow price of social security benefits would be expected to reduce the level of benefits provided. A related point, however, is that demand is affected not only by price but also by income, and with rising income people may wish to have more leisure, including spending a greater percentage of their life in retirement.

The question can be raised as to whether the law of downward-sloping demand applies to social security benefits, since they are not purchased in the marketplace, but are determined through the forces of politics and public policy. Ultimately that is an empirical question that has received little attention, but the theory that this law does apply to social security benefits has received some confirmation (Turner 1984).

Between 1970 and 2000, the growth rates in Social Security–covered workers and beneficiaries in the United States were roughly equal, implying no change in the dependency ratio. However, between 2000 and 2030, according to the intermediate projection of the Social Security Administration actuaries, the number of beneficiaries will grow considerably faster than the number of covered workers (Table 3.1). That change places pressure on Social Security financing and thus strengthens the case for adopting an automatic adjustment mechanism.

## AUTOMATIC ADJUSTMENT MECHANISMS

Recognizing the political risks for politicians and workers of resolving social security insolvency through ad hoc reforms, at least 12 countries have adopted life-expectancy indexing of social security benefits or automatic adjustments tied to an indicator of social security insolvency. Both types of reforms provide automatic adjustment mechanisms for sustaining the solvency of social security systems. With life-expectancy indexing of benefits, taxes, or the early or normal

**Table 3.1  Projected Percentage Change in Old-Age and Survivors Insurance (OASI)–Covered Workers and Beneficiaries, Selected Periods, 1970–2030**

| Year | OASI-covered workers (000s) | OASI beneficiaries (000s) | Ratio of beneficiaries to covered workers (%) |
|---|---|---|---|
| 1970 | 92,788 | 22,618 | 24.4 |
| 2000 | 154,624 | 38,556 | 24.9 |
| 2030 (intermediate projection) | 184,794 | 71,547 | 38.7 |
| Percentage change | | | |
| 1970–2000 | 66.6 | 70.5 | 2.0 |
| 2000–2030 | 55.0 | 85.6 | 55.4 |

SOURCE: Author's calculations from Social Security Board of Trustees (2008).

retirement age, increases in life expectancy automatically lead to program parameter changes. However, the adjustment mechanisms used for indexing can vary.

Six issues need to be considered in analyzing automatic adjustment mechanisms:

### 1) The frequency of the adjustment

Some automatic adjustments test for the need for change and make any necessary changes annually; these adjustments are designed as part of the ongoing financing to maintain the solvency of a system. For example, life-expectancy indexing of initial benefits generally is done annually, as in Sweden, but Italy adjusts benefits every three years.

### 2) The triggering event

The choice of triggering event has varied. Some adjustments are tied to the social security system's underlying economics and demographics, such as changes in life expectancy, the dependency ratio, or real wages. Others are tied to a measure of the insolvency of the system, and adjustments are made only if the system is judged not to be solvent over the long run.

### 3) Whether the trigger is a hard trigger or a soft trigger

The trigger can be a "soft" trigger, meaning that the government is obligated to do something, but may choose among different measures. Alternatively, it can be a "hard" trigger, meaning that the adjustment is automatic (Penner and Steuerle 2007). In most countries adopting automatic adjustment mechanisms, the trigger is a hard trigger if the adjustment involves life-expectancy indexing of benefits. However, triggers tied to a measure of insolvency are sometimes soft triggers, with some degree of political involvement in the process. Even in Sweden, discussed later, which has a hard trigger with respect to insolvency, the government maintains oversight, so the automatic adjustment may be overridden.

### 4) Whether retirees or workers, or both, are affected

The intergenerational effects of an adjustment can differ. In some countries retirees are considered particularly vulnerable and are exempt from benefit reductions, with workers bearing the full cost of the adjustment. In other countries, both retirees and workers are affected by the automatic adjustments.

### 5) The change that is triggered

The change that is triggered can be an adjustment in tax rates, current or future benefits, retirement ages, or other parameters, such as the number of years counted in the benefit calculation.

### 6) The extent of advance notice of a change

The change can take place immediately, with little or no advance notice, or it can take place with a number of years of advance notice.

### Indexing for Life Expectancy: Shifting Risk to Retirees

Starting in the late 1990s, a number of countries, but not the United States, have reformed their social security systems to incorporate life-expectancy indexing or other automatic adjustments. Life-expectancy indexing is the policy of adjusting some parameter of social security, such as benefits, taxes, the early retirement age, or the normal retirement age, for changes in life expectancy. While the costs of social security benefits presumably are ultimately borne by both workers and retirees, life-expectancy indexing determines in advance how the distribution of those costs will be borne.

## Indexing Benefits

Defined contribution pension systems use life-expectancy indexing when they annuitize benefits based on current life expectancy. This feature of defined contribution systems can be incorporated into social security benefit systems by life-expectancy indexing of their benefits. Life-expectancy indexing of benefits automatically reduces annual benefits to offset the increase in lifetime benefits that accompanies an increase in life expectancy. With life-expectancy indexing of benefits, retirees are still protected from their individual (idiosyncratic) life-expectancy risk because they receive benefits as long as they live. Individual or idiosyncratic life-expectancy risk is the risk that individuals will live longer than the average for their cohort.

Life-expectancy indexing of benefits gradually lowers the replacement rate—the ratio of earnings in the period before retirement to benefits received at retirement. Life-expectancy indexing results in reduced annual benefits (but not lifetime benefits) relative to earnings. Thus, over time, the generosity of the social security system, measured by the replacement rate, is reduced. With increased life expectancy, working longer is a desirable policy outcome for many people who are able and willing to do so. For anyone who chooses and is able to do so, reductions in social security benefits could be offset by working longer.

Countries have used a couple of methods to index benefits for changes in life expectancy. One method adjusts for the percentage increase in life expectancy. For example, if life expectancy at retirement age increases by 1 percent, benefits would be reduced by 1 percent. Portugal and Japan use this method.

A more commonly used method adjusts for the percentage increase in the present value of benefits caused by the increase in life expectancy. For example, if an increase in life expectancy raises the expected present value of benefits at retirement by 1 percent, annual benefits would be reduced by 1 percent. With the interest discounting of future benefits (because of the time value of money), an increase in life expectancy of 1 percent raises the expected present value of benefits by less than 1 percent because the increased benefits are received years in the future. For that reason, the second method of indexing results in a smaller reduction of benefits for a given increase in life expectancy than the first method.

## Indexing Retirement Ages

Alternatively, retirement ages can be indexed. Life-expectancy indexing of the normal retirement age (for full benefits) and the early retirement age (eligibility age) has two dimensions:

1) The level of benefits received at the new retirement age

2) The increase in early or normal retirement age

The first dimension of retirement-age indexing is the level of benefits received at the new retirement age. The level or amount of benefits can be the same as that payable at the former age. For example, if the age were raised from 62 to 63, the benefits formerly receivable at 62 would be receivable at 63. With this approach, indexing the earliest retirement age in Social Security would reduce benefit costs because workers would receive the same level of annual benefits, but for fewer years. The replacement rate would be unaffected by that adjustment, but would generally be raised if the worker worked an additional year.

Alternatively, the level of benefits can be raised for those retiring at age 62 to reflect the adjustment for postponed retirement. The benefits receivable at 63 would be the same as the benefits receivable at 63 under the former eligibility age. Thus, there would be no effect on the benefits of people retiring at ages 63 or higher. This method of indexing the earliest retirement age would have little effect on benefit costs in the United States because the increased benefits with postponed retirement offset the effect of the reduced number of years that benefits would be received.

The second dimension of indexing retirement ages is the increase of either the eligibility age or the normal retirement age, or both. For example, either age could increase one year for every year's increase in life expectancy, or it could increase at a rate that would maintain a constant ratio of retirement years to working years. Alternatively, the increase could be set to maintain a constant ratio of beneficiaries to workers (dependency ratio) (Gebhardtsbauer 1998).

The different ways in which the eligibility age or the normal retirement age can be indexed to life expectancy have different effects on social security financing. With indexing to maintain a constant life expectancy at the retirement age, the costs of the social security system will decline over time because the ratio of beneficiaries to workers will tend to decline (Gebhardtsbauer 1998).

With life-expectancy indexing to maintain a constant ratio of retirement years to working years, because the length of the retirement period increases over time, the expected present value of benefits rises with increases in life expectancy. However, keeping the ratio of the retirement period to the working period constant and setting the benefit level so that the benefits at the new age equal those receivable at the old age insulates the social security system from adverse financial effects due to increasing life expectancy. If maintaining a constant ratio of work years to retirement years also maintains a constant ratio of workers to retirees, there would be no change in the old-age dependency ratio, and the system's solvency would be unaffected by changes in life expectancy. However, life-expectancy indexing done this way is not sufficient to maintain a constant payroll tax rate when the retirement of an exceptionally large age cohort looms, such as the baby boom generation, since such a shift has a major impact on the old-age dependency ratio, and thus on the cost of providing benefits.

## INTERNATIONAL EXPERIENCE WITH AUTOMATIC ADJUSTMENT MECHANISMS

This section surveys the experience of high-income countries that have automatic adjustment mechanisms to maintain social security solvency. It investigates how these mechanisms work. The details of the international experience are provided because they yield valuable insights as to how such policies might be implemented and how they would work in the United States.

The countries that have these mechanisms can be divided into four groups. First, traditional pay-as-you-go systems that have instituted life-expectancy indexing of benefits are considered. Second, countries that use life-expectancy indexing of the earliest age at which social security benefits can be received are reviewed. Third, countries are considered that automatically adjust other parameters of their social security systems, such as the number of years for full benefits. And fourth, countries with automatic adjustment mechanisms that are tied to solvency are considered.

## 1) Life-Expectancy Indexing in Traditional Pay-as-You-Go Social Security Programs

Life-expectancy indexing of benefits can be incorporated within the framework of a traditional pay-as-you-go social security system, such as the U.S. system. Finland, Norway, and Portugal have done so.

**Finland.** In 2003, Finland passed a law to incorporate increases in life expectancy into the calculation of social security benefits. The law took effect in 2010. As in other countries adopting life-expectancy indexing, the life-expectancy adjustment uses unisex mortality tables, thus ignoring gender (or other) differences in life expectancy.

Because of year-to-year fluctuations in mortality rates, countries using life-expectancy indexing generally average mortality rates over several years, which smoothes out the yearly fluctuations. Finland uses mortality tables based on past mortality data averaged over a five-year period to adjust initial pension benefits at age 62. Thus, in the first year, the average life expectancy at age 62 for the years 2004–2008 was compared to the average for the years 2003–2007.

The life-expectancy adjustment for an individual's benefits depends on the person's year of birth. A person's benefits at retirement are adjusted for unisex life expectancy at age 62 for that birth cohort, without regard to the person's age at retirement. Thus, two persons retiring at ages 62 and 63 but born in the same year would have the same percentage reduction in their annual benefits. Of course, the person retiring at age 63 would receive a larger benefit because of the benefit adjustment for postponement of retirement.

Life-expectancy indexing in Finland is done so that increases in life expectancy do not raise the expected present value of lifetime social security benefits. The indexing is based on the amount that an increase in life expectancy would increase the expected present value of benefits. A 2 percent discount rate is used to calculate the annuity value. Disability pensions are also adjusted this way (Alho, Lassila, and Valkonen 2006; Lindell 2003). By 2040, after 30 years of life-expectancy indexing, the level of benefits is expected to be reduced to 89 percent of the level without indexing, or a reduction of less than 0.4 percent per year (Whitehouse 2007a).

**Portugal.** In 2006, Portugal passed legislation that indexes its social security benefits for improvements in life expectancy. The legislation took effect in 2008. The reduction of benefits is based directly on the percentage change in life expectancy, rather than on the percentage change in the expected value of pension benefits arising because of the improvement in life-expectancy (Whitehouse 2007b).

## 2) Indexing the Eligibility Age for Improvements in Life Expectancy

Rather than indexing benefits, the eligibility age to receive benefits can be indexed for improvements in life expectancy.

**United Kingdom.** A British pension commission proposed life-expectancy indexing of the earliest age at which workers are eligible to receive social security benefits (Pensions Commission 2005). The commission was chaired by Adair Turner, now Lord Turner, and was informally known as the Turner Commission. The early retirement age in 2009 was 65 for men and 60 for women, but starting in 2010 it was scheduled to rise to 65 for women by 2020. The British proposal would index the eligibility age so that the ratio of working years to retirement years would be constant. It would announce any increase in the eligibility age 15 years in advance. Thus, for the current age of 65 for men, no one aged 50 or older would be affected. Based on the projection of life expectancy improvements, such indexing would result in an early retirement age of 68 in 2050. The Pensions Commission argues that this type of indexing would be fair across generations because every generation would spend roughly the same proportion of adult life in retirement.

With this proposal, the eligibility age would not increase one-to-one with increases in life expectancy. Rather, if the ratio of retirement years to working years is one to two, then for every three years' increase in life expectancy, the eligibility age would increase by two years to maintain the ratio of one retirement year for every two working years.

The British Parliament modified the Turner Commission proposal. The law Parliament enacted raises the eligibility age in three steps. The eligibility age first increases between April 2024 and April 2026 from 65 to 66, followed by a phase-in from April 2034 to 2036 of the increase from 66 to 67, and a phase-in from April 2044 to 2046 of the increase from 67 to 68 (Watson Wyatt Worldwide 2007). This reform is not indexing because the increases are not linked to actual increases in life expectancy. However, it could be called quasi indexing because the increases are linked to projected increases in life expectancy.

**Denmark.** As of 2010, Denmark was the only country to enact legislation to index the social security benefit eligibility age to increases in life expectancy. This change takes effect with a long delay. Denmark provides two old-age social security benefits. First, the early retirement pension benefit requires the recipient to have worked a certain number of years in Denmark. Denmark will raise the eligibility age for that benefit by six months each year from 2019 to 2022, so that the early retirement eligibility age increases from 60 to 62.

The second old-age benefit program is a universal old-age pension that is available based on a person's years of residence in Denmark. It has no work history requirement. The eligibility age for this universal old-age pension will rise by six months each year from 2024 to 2027, so that the universal pension eligibility age increases from 65 to 67. From then, increases in the eligibility age for both benefit programs will be tied to increases in life expectancy. The life expectancy review is supposed to be done every five years (the first review is scheduled for 2015), and the change in retirement age will take effect after a notice period of 15 years. The Danish parliament must approve every increase in the retirement age. By 2045, the eligibility age is expected to reach 68.3 years (Whitehouse 2007b). The goal is for the early retirement age to be raised so that life expectancy from that age, measured at age 60, will be 19.5 years. Thus, the Danish reform does not split the increased life expectancy between the working years and retirement years but fully raises the eligibility age for increases in life expectancy.

### 3) Indexing Years of Contributions Required for a Full Benefit

Other parameters of the social security benefit calculation can be indexed, such as the years of contributions required for a full benefit.

**France.** In 2008, French workers needed 40 years of contributions to receive full social security benefits. Starting in 2009, that number has increased by one calendar quarter per year and will continue to do so until it reaches 41 years in 2012. This change will reduce social security benefits by about 2.5 percent for people working 40 years. Thereafter, through 2020, the contribution period for full benefits will increase as needed to keep the ratio of the contribution period to the average retirement period equal to its ratio in 2003, which was approximately two to one.[2] The ratio is measured as the number of years required for a full pension for work starting at age 20, divided by the expected duration of retirement.

This adjustment mechanism effectively results in a reduction in benefits that is tied to increases in life expectancy. The French government retains the right to forgo these adjustments if weak labor market conditions do not make it feasible for workers to work the extra years.

### 4) Countries with Automatic Adjustment Mechanisms Tied to Solvency

Some countries have adopted automatic adjustment mechanisms tied to measures of the solvency of their social security program.

**Sweden.** Sweden is a leader in the movement toward automatic adjustments of social security. For that reason its system is explained in greater detail than for other countries that have followed its lead. In 1994, the Swedish parliament passed legislation establishing the principles of the reform. This was followed by a series of implementing laws passed starting in 1998 that established a Notional Defined Contribution (NDC) system, alongside a mandatory, fully funded individual account plan. The legislation for the automatic balancing mechanism in the NDC plan was passed in 2001. That system is financed by a combined employer-employee tax rate of 16 percent of wages (Table 3.2). Each worker has a notional account to which contributions are credited.

**Table 3.2 Sweden: Changes in Contributions and Benefits**

| System parameter | Value (%) |
|---|---|
| Contributions: employer-employee tax rate | |
| Rate in 2010 | 16 |
| Future rate | 16 |
| Benefits: replacement rate (avg. worker) | |
| Rate in 2008 | 53 |
| Future rate (2050) | 40 |

NOTE: The replacement rate includes both the NDC pension and the mandatory individual account pension.
SOURCE: Swedish Ministry of Health and Social Affairs (2005).

The accumulated account balance is credited each year with a rate of return equal to the growth rate of average wages.[3] In addition, 2.5 percent of wages up to a ceiling are paid to the individual account plan, called the premium pension.

Each year, because of life-expectancy indexing of benefits, the initial benefits received by new beneficiaries are adjusted downward as a new birth cohort reaches the eligibility age of 61 (Table 3.3). The life-expectancy indexing of the system started in 1995, before the NDC system actually began. It is expected that by approximately 2032, after nearly 40 years of indexing, workers would need to postpone retirement by two years and seven months to avoid receiving lower benefits in

**Table 3.3 Sweden: Life-Expectancy Indexing of Benefits**

| (1) Birth cohort | (2) Reaches age 65 in | (3) Life expectancy at age 65 | (4) Retirement age required to neutralize the effect on benefits of increased life expectancy | (5) Implying an expected length of retirement (col. 3 minus col. 4) |
|---|---|---|---|---|
| 1930 | 1995 | 82 yrs. 5 mos. | 65 yrs. 0 mos. | 17 yrs. 5 mos. |
| 1940 | 2005 | 83 yrs. 7 mos. | 65 yrs. 9 mos. | 17 yrs. 10 mos. |
| 1950 | 2015 | 84 yrs. 10 mos. | 66 yrs. 7 mos. | 18 yrs. 3 mos. |
| 1960 | 2025 | 85 yrs. 7 mos. | 67 yrs. 2 mos. | 18 yrs. 5 mos. |
| 1970 | 2035 | 86 yrs. 3 mos. | 67 yrs. 7 mos. | 18 yrs. 8 mos. |

SOURCE: Swedish Social Insurance Agency (2005).

comparison to the benefits they would have received had there been no indexing. Thus, people formerly retiring at age 63 would need to retire at 65 years and 7 months to receive the same level of benefits as without the benefit reduction.

Life-expectancy indexing of benefits is done by an adjustment that reflects improvements in life expectancy at age 65. No further adjustments to retirees' benefits are made for improvements in mortality after age 65.

The Swedish system uses period mortality tables, which are based on the experience of a cross section of older persons, not projecting future mortality improvements. For example, period tables would be based on the mortality experience of the population alive in the year 2000, rather than the expected experience of people aged 61 in that year, projecting into the future. For each cohort, the annuity divisor adjustment—the amount by which the worker's accumulated balance is divided to determine the worker's initial benefit—is established at age 65, with a provisional adjustment made for retirements starting at age 61, which is the eligibility age.

In establishing adjustment mechanisms, a fundamental question is whether any of the adjustment will be borne by current retirees. Generally, U.S. Social Security reform proposals exempt current retirees and workers nearing retirement age on the grounds that people in those age groups have limited ability to change their work and savings plans to adjust to reforms. Sweden has not adopted that principle.

In Sweden, if the growth rate of real per capita wages is constant at 1.6 percent per year, the social security annuity is adjusted solely by changes in the Consumer Price Index (CPI). However, if the annual growth rate of real per capita wage income in Sweden falls below 1.6 percent, the cost-of-living adjustment is less than the increase in the CPI, and if the growth rate of real per capita wage income exceeds 1.6 percent, the adjustment is greater than the CPI. For example, if the annual growth rate in real per capita wages was 1.5 percent, the increase in benefits in payment would be the rate of growth of the CPI minus 0.1 percent, which would cause a slight decline in the real level of benefits paid.

Real per capita wage growth in Sweden has averaged about 2 percent a year over long periods (Palmer 2000). Because this average rate exceeds the rate of 1.6 percent in the adjustment formula, over time this indexing is expected to be more generous than price indexing. Thus, Swedish pensioners share with workers in the fluctuations in the Swedish economy and in the long-term growth of the economy. However, in an economic recession, as occurred in 2009–2010, indexed benefits of Swedish pensioners are increased by less than the level provided by price indexing.

Life-expectancy indexing and the adjustment of benefits in payment for changes in productivity may at times be inadequate to assure solvency. To handle this, Sweden has built into its system a mechanism called the automatic balancing mechanism. This adjustment mechanism has two goals: 1) to set the contribution rate so that there will be no need to raise it in the future and 2) to automatically restore financial balance to the social security system without the intervention of politicians. The automatic balancing mechanism is used when the system is not fully solvent in the long run.

To determine whether it needs to implement the automatic balancing mechanism, each year the Swedish government measures the assets and liabilities of its social security system. The assets in the system are measured as the assets in the associated trust fund, called a buffer fund, plus the estimated present value of future contributions. If the present value of liabilities for future benefits exceeds the value of assets, adjustments are made to reduce future benefits. Specifically, the adjustment mechanism reduces the rate of return used to calculate accruals in the notional balances below the rate of growth of average real wages.[4] It also reduces by the same amount the indexing rate for benefits in payment. For example, if a shortfall of assets to liabilities of 5 percent develops, the current benefit accruals of workers and the benefits in payment would be reduced by 5 percent. Thus, both workers and retirees are affected by the adjustment. The level of contributions is not affected.

When the system is in good financial condition, workers can be assured that these cuts will not occur in the near future. However, if the system is near the point where adjustments may be made, workers and retirees face uncertainty as to whether cuts will occur within the next few years. This mechanism shares the burden of the adjustment across generations. However, if cuts are made and the trigger later is switched off because conditions have again become more favorable, those who were working during the adjustment phase will not be affected at all:

the value of their accumulated pension rights will be restored. The pensioners affected by the balancing mechanism, on the contrary, will not receive any compensation for what they lost during the period when the balancing mechanism was active.

The logic of the system dictates that the adjustment occurs through accrual and benefit reductions, but not through tax rate changes. If the payroll tax rate were increased, that would increase the contributions credited to the individual accounts, which would increase future benefit liabilities, and thus would not help restore solvency.[5]

Because of the fall in world stock markets in 2008, the reserve funds for the Swedish Notional Defined Contribution (NDC) system fell considerably in value. The buffer funds received a negative return of −21 percent (Sundén 2009). Balance is restored by reducing per capita wage indexation of earned pension rights for current workers and reducing the indexation of benefits for current retirees. The adjustment occurs with a lag, so the 4.5 percent scheduled increase in pension benefits in 2009 was not affected by the financial crisis. Because of slow wage growth, benefits were scheduled to decrease by 1.3 percent. But, as a result of the automatic adjustment mechanism, benefits were scheduled to decrease by a further 3.3 percent in 2010, or a total of 4.6 percent. The cuts would continue until the system regained financial balance.[6] With current projections, the outlook improves only after 2012. Any surpluses that occur after balancing are used to increase indexation until the value of pension credits and benefits are restored.

The proposed cuts generated an immediate response from the five Swedish political parties that support the pension reform. They proposed a change in the procedure for valuing buffer fund assets from market value to a three-year average in order to smooth the pattern. The government decided to go forward with the change. As a result, the response of the NDC plan financing to the economic recession will be muted, and it should take longer for the system to return to balance. Instead of a reduction in benefits of 4.5 percent in 2010, the reduction was 3.0 percent. That means that if inflation is 3 percent, there will be a real reduction in benefits of 6 percent. In 2011, instead of a nominal reduction in benefits of 1.7 percent, the reduction will be 2.8 percent. And in 2012, instead of a projected increase in nominal benefits of 0.8 percent, nominal benefits will be reduced by 0.5 percent (Sundén 2009).

While these changes modify the original adjustment mechanism, substantial cuts in real benefits still occur over a short period, as real benefits decline by approximately 12 percent over two years and 16 percent over three years, assuming a 3 percent inflation rate.

A criticism of the Swedish system is that, because of its automatic adjustments, its replacement rate is falling over time. That criticism is addressed for low-wage workers in Sweden by the provision of a minimum benefit. Beneficiaries with relatively low benefits also receive the guarantee benefit. About 43 percent of beneficiaries receive that benefit (Sundén 2009). When the NDC benefits are cut by the automatic adjustments, the benefit from the guarantee benefit is increased, somewhat offsetting the cut for the retirees receiving the guarantee benefit.

At some point, however, Sweden may decide it needs to raise its early retirement age, which is relatively low at 61. Raising the early retirement age would allow Sweden to raise the replacement rate because higher benefits would be received, but for fewer years.

The Swedish public, after its limited experience with the NDC system, appears to have readily accepted the Swedish system. The lack of widespread criticism may be because the replacement rate is declining slowly, so the public may have limited awareness of the long-run decline in the replacement rate. Also, acceptance of the system could diminish when the automatic adjustment mechanism is used to reduce accruals and the price indexing of benefits.

**Germany.** Unlike Sweden, Germany does not index social security benefits for life expectancy. It, however, has changed the calculation of benefits to incorporate life expectancy as one aspect of a more complex adjustment mechanism. The adjustment mechanism is called the sustainability factor. The sustainability factor, which was introduced in 2004 and took effect in 2005, attempts to achieve sustainability by limiting the growth rate of average benefits (Table 3.4). The sustainability factor incorporates not only life-expectancy changes but all demographic factors that affect the dependency ratio (Toft 2007). It includes the effects of changes in migration, birth rates, labor force participation rates, and retirement rates. It is used to index benefits, but part of the adjustment to solvency also raises the social security payroll tax rate.

Initial benefits for a retiree are determined by multiplying the benefits received under the benefit formula of the previous year by the

**Table 3.4  Germany: Changes in Contributions and Benefits**

| System parameter | Value (%) |
|---|---|
| Contributions: employer-employee tax rate | |
| Rate in 2008 | 19.5 |
| Future rate (2030) | 22.0 |
| Benefits: replacement rate (avg. worker) | |
| Rate in 2008 | 70.0 |
| Future rate | 64.0 |

SOURCE: Toft (2007).

sustainability factor. The sustainability factor is based on the percentage change in the dependency ratio.[7]

A safety clause, however, sets a limit on the adjustment so that nominal benefits cannot be reduced. Without this clause, nominal benefits could be reduced during a period of low earnings growth or declining earnings, as occurred in Sweden. The safety clause took effect immediately in Germany, limiting the effect of the sustainability factor in 2005 and 2006 (Toft 2007).

The sustainability factor has reduced the projected payroll tax rate necessary to finance the system in 2040 from 28 percent to 24 percent (Capretta 2006). Germany's goal is to limit the payroll tax rate to no higher than 20 percent by 2020 and 22 percent by 2030 (Penner and Steuerle 2007). The sustainability factor is weighted so that it offsets just one-quarter of the percentage increase in the system's dependency ratio, rather than the full increase. The difference is made up by the projected increase in payroll taxes.

Germany uses a points system for calculating social security benefits. In that system, contributing for one year at the average wage earns a worker one point. A retiree's benefits are based on the total number of points earned by the retiree multiplied by a factor measuring the value of a point. The sustainability factor affects the value of a point, so it affects both current and future retirees. Thus, the benefits of retirees are affected by the adjustment, as in Sweden.

**Japan.** Japan has studied the reforms in Sweden and Germany and developed its own system of automatic adjustments that incorporates features from both countries. Japan calls its approach modified indexation.

Japan's social security program has had to deal with increasing life expectancy at older ages that is among the highest in the world. In addition, it has faced a continuing decline in the birth rate to below the rate that would be sufficient to maintain the population at its current level. Because of the low birth rate and limited immigration, Japan's population and workforce are both declining.

Even though Japan passed major social security reform legislation in 2000, greater-than-expected improvement in life expectancy, plus greater-than-expected decline in the birth rate, caused the need for further reform in 2004. Because of the political cost to politicians of the repeated process of making unpopular social security reforms, Japanese politicians wanted an automatic mechanism that would return the system to solvency without their continued intervention (Sakamoto 2005).

As in the United States, so in Japan, Sweden, and Germany there is a desire to not raise the payroll tax rate above a set level. In Japan, Sweden, and Germany that desire motivated the introduction of the automatic adjustment. Japan decided to introduce the adjustment in part because younger workers were concerned about the possibility of high contribution rates, which they viewed as unfair to their generation.

In reform legislation passed in 2004, Japan incorporated a demographic factor into the calculation of social security benefits (Sakamoto 2008; Takayama 2006). The social security adjustment reduces the indexing of initial benefits and benefits in subsequent years.

The Japanese government is gradually increasing the payroll tax rate for its social security program, called the Employees' Pension Insurance Scheme, to 18.3 percent in 2017. At that point, the payroll tax rate is considered to be fixed, with no further increases necessary (Table 3.5). In the absence of the 2004 reforms, the payroll tax rate was projected to increase to 25.9 percent. It was 13.58 percent in 2004.

With these increases in the payroll tax rate, it is estimated under the best-case scenario that the modified indexation will continue until 2023, when indexation will return to that used in 2004.[8] In the Japanese social security system, initial benefits grow at the rate of growth of disposable income. Under the automatic adjustment mechanism, the indexing of initial benefits at retirement is reduced until financial solvency is restored.

The reduction factor takes into account the decline in the number of people in the Japanese workforce and the increase in life expectancy.

**Table 3.5  Japan: Changes in Contributions and Benefits**

| System parameter | Value (%) |
|---|---|
| Contributions: employer-employee tax rate | |
| Rate in 2008 | 15.35 |
| Future rate (2017) | 18.30 |
| Benefits: replacement rate (avg. worker) | |
| Rate in 2008 | 59.00 |
| Future rate (2023) | 50.00 |

SOURCE: Sakamoto (2008); Takayama (2006).

The factor equals the rate of decline in the Japanese workforce participating in social security programs plus the rate of increase in life expectancy at age 65.

Japanese policy experts have noted that the growth rate of the beneficiary population also affects solvency. However, they took a long-term perspective and did not incorporate that into the calculation, since the growth rate of the beneficiary population would eventually reflect the growth rate of the workforce (Sakamoto 2005).

For the benefit calculation, the projected rate of increase in life expectancy at age 65 is fixed in the law at 0.3 percent annually, or approximately three weeks a year. That adjustment is based on the 2002 projection over the period from 2000 to 2025. Thus, this indexation can be categorized as quasi indexing because it is not tied to actual changes in life expectancy. It was fixed in advance to avoid year-to-year fluctuations in the benefit adjustment and to set the benefit adjustment so that Japanese workers would be able to know in advance the change that would affect their benefits.

It is expected that the demographic factor will reduce the indexation rate for benefits at retirement by 0.9 percentage points per year on average, compared to the previous method. By reducing the growth rate of benefits to less than the growth rate in real wages, this change is projected to reduce the average replacement rate from 59 percent in 2008 to 50 percent by 2023.

The adjustment factor, however, is not applied if it would cause nominal benefits to decline, as in Germany. If the Consumer Price Index declines in a year (which has happened in Japan and in the United States) or if per capita disposable income declines, benefits are maintained at their nominal value, rather than being cut to reflect the effects of indexing.

Also, if the replacement rate fell much more rapidly than expected, and fell to 50 percent or lower, the adjustment mechanism would be stopped, and the policy would be reviewed. Thus, the law contains a provision to override the automatic stabilizer. This provision is known as the minimum benefit provision.

**Canada.** Canada uses an approach to automatic adjustments that differs from Sweden, Germany, and Japan. Canada introduced its automatic adjustment mechanism in 1997.

The Canada Pension Plan (CPP) is the main social security program for Canada, except for the province of Quebec, which maintains a similar but separate plan—the Quebec Pension Plan. These two plans operate on top of a flat benefit. The CPP is a hybrid between a pay-as-you-go system and a fully funded system. It is partially funded, but, unlike the U.S. Social Security system, it is not projected to run out of money. Benefits are designed to replace 25 percent of the worker's average wages into the future, and thus grow over time for successive cohorts at the growth rate of average wages (Table 3.6).

The payroll tax rate is projected to be sufficiently higher than the rate necessary to maintain pay-as-you-go funding for a number of years, so the trust fund will continue to grow over time. The CPP is financed with a combined employee-employer tax rate of 9.9 percent. Its fund is invested partially in world stock markets. The system is designed so that the fund will be adequate to pay for the retirement benefits of the Canadian baby boomers and to cover the aging of the population. There

**Table 3.6  Canada: Changes in Contributions and Benefits**

| System parameter | Value (%) |
|---|---|
| Contributions: employer-employee tax rate | |
|   Rate in 2008 | 9.9 |
|   Future rate | 9.9 |
| Benefits: replacement rate (avg. worker) | |
|   Rate in 2008 | 25.0 |
|   Future rate | 25.0 |

SOURCE: Office of the Superintendent of Financial Institutions Canada (2007).

should be no need for further contribution rate increases or benefit cuts. However, if financial markets are weak for a prolonged period or if life expectancy increases considerably more rapidly than anticipated, or if another economic or demographic variable affecting funding turns out to be much more adverse to funding than expected, an adjustment may be needed.

Every three years, the system's chief actuary evaluates the CPP's financial sustainability. If the chief actuary determines that the system is not financially sustainable in the long run, legislation requires an automatic adjustment (Office of the Superintendent of Financial Institutions Canada 2007). However, the automatic adjustment takes effect only if the Canadian provincial finance ministers cannot first decide on an adjustment of their own—an outcome that is considered unlikely.

If the automatic adjustment takes effect, it freezes benefit indexation for three years, eliminating cost-of-living increases for retirees during that period. In addition, the automatic adjustment increases the contribution rate over that three-year period by an amount equal to half of the adjustment needed to reach the new long-term contribution rate required to restore solvency. That rate is maintained until the next triennial evaluation. Thus, the changes are borne both through an increase in contributions and a reduction in benefits in payment (Brown 2008). If changes in long-run assumptions raise the projected steady-state contribution rate required to maintain a constant ratio of assets to expenditures, the contribution rate will be increased permanently.

The Canadian social security system has been designed so that there is little need for the adjustment mechanism. By moving toward partial funding, the system is designed to maintain both a constant payroll tax rate across age cohorts and a constant replacement rate. This is a degree of long-run stability that few social security systems have achieved.

## COMPARING THE OPTIONS: THE PROS AND CONS

Life-expectancy indexing of benefits results in a falling replacement rate over time when measured at a fixed retirement age. For this reason, social security will provide a decreasingly generous benefit over time as traditionally measured by the replacement rate concept.

Working longer can offset this effect by raising a person's benefits. Alternatively, workers not wishing to work longer could increase their savings for retirement, though the evidence of widespread undersaving for retirement suggests that this approach would not be popular.

Any system with a declining replacement rate, such as the Swedish system, eventually will reach the point where the replacement rate is politically unacceptable, and further reform will be necessary. Thus, a system that achieves solvency with a declining replacement rate does not prevent the need for future reforms. The outcome of future reforms is subject to the usual political risks as to timing and distributional consequences.

One Swedish commentator (Scherman 2007) is highly critical of the decline in replacement rates that will result from the Swedish reform. He argues that the early retirement age should be raised to offset the decline, and that the payroll tax rate should not be considered permanently fixed. Furthermore, he advocates reinstituting a "normal pension age" to clarify to the general public what retirement age is needed to obtain a "decent" pension. Moreover, he calls for an in-depth discussion of how the labor market reacts to the need for offering employment opportunities at an advanced age.

Life-expectancy indexing of benefits preserves the option of receiving social security benefits at an early age. That said, some people who retire at the early retirement age, particularly those with long life expectancy, probably would be financially better off if they postponed retirement to a higher age, when they would receive higher benefits. People generally will receive higher annual social security benefits if the early retirement age is indexed than if pension benefits are indexed, because pensioners will receive the benefits starting at a later age and for fewer years.

Indexing the eligibility age has the added feature of encouraging people to work longer. However, not everyone is able to do so. People with long careers in physically demanding jobs and people in poor health may be unable to postpone their retirement. Options could be provided to meet the needs of these people. For example, the eligibility age could be maintained at its current level for people with long careers or for people with low lifetime average earnings. The eligibility requirements for disability benefits could be eased for people above a certain age but below the social security eligibility age.

Indexing can also be compared to quasi indexing. With quasi indexing, instead of relating policy changes to actual changes in life expectancy, such policy changes could be linked to projected changes in life expectancy, as in Japan. An argument in favor of indexing is that if life expectancy improves more slowly than anticipated, the system automatically adjusts to the new reality, and smaller reductions in benefits are made. However, indexing creates uncertainty as to when changes in social security will occur and how large they will be. With quasi indexing, a schedule of changes is announced in advance so that, for example, people would know far in advance the early retirement age or the benefit reduction that would be relevant for their birth cohort.

## DISTRIBUTIONAL CONSEQUENCES

The options have different consequences as to the distribution of resources across people with different characteristics. Distributional issues can be addressed across the income distribution within a given age cohort and across age cohorts. A reform that raises the eligibility age will have relatively less effect on workers who already are postponing retirement past the eligibility age. That group includes high-income workers who find considerable nonpecuniary, as well as pecuniary, rewards from their work. It also includes low-income workers who continue to work because they need the money.

While the adjustments in benefits resulting from indexing generally produce an across-the-board cut in benefits, their effects on retirees would differ across the income distribution. For example, a 5 percent cut in benefits due to life-expectancy indexing of benefits would leave the distribution of benefits the same across income classes. However, it would affect the distribution of income because lower-income persons tend to rely more on social security benefits, so their income would fall by a greater percentage than the income of higher-income persons.

Indexing the early retirement age may be more favorable to lower-income workers than indexing benefits, provided other changes are made to help lower-income people who are unable to extend their working lives. However, if benefits are indexed, it may be less likely that those changes in other programs would be made.

The different options for social security reform also have different distributional consequences across age cohorts. Automatic adjustment mechanisms designed to maintain the solvency of social security tend to result in smaller changes made over a longer period of time and affect more age cohorts than changes made to restore solvency when insolvency is impending.

Life-expectancy varies across racial groups. Where there is racial diversity within the population, such as in the United States, life-expectancy indexing of the eligibility age raises the question of whether this policy would be fair to all racial groups. The effects on different racial groups with different life expectancies and different risks of disability depend in part on whether disability benefits would also be subject to life-expectancy indexing of benefits. If disability benefits were not also life-expectancy indexed, groups that have a higher take-up rate for those benefits, such as blacks, would be treated relatively favorably since those benefits would not be reduced.

All countries with life-expectancy indexing use unisex life expectancy rather than having different indexing for men and women or for other identifiable groups (such as race) with different mortality rates. If life expectancy improved at different rates for different demographic groups, indexing that was based on the average for all groups might be unfair to some groups. Singh and Siahpush (2006), among others, have documented a widening of the mortality gap by socioeconomic status. In this situation, less than full indexing might be desirable. If life-expectancy indexing were seen to adversely affect low-income groups, that effect could be offset by increasing the progressivity of social security benefits through changes in the benefit formula.

## INDEXING OPTIONS FOR U.S. SOCIAL SECURITY

Life-expectancy indexing of U.S. Social Security benefits could be structured several ways. Benefits received at age 62 could be reduced. That approach was proposed by the President's Commission to Strengthen Social Security (2001), which recommended that benefits be adjusted every 10 years. Another option would be to index the eligibility age and the normal retirement age so that the eligibility age was a fixed number of years earlier than the normal retirement age. This type of indexing would result in a smaller reduction in benefits than under life-expectancy indexing of benefits because the increase in the eligibility age would offset the benefit reduction. The legislated increases in the normal retirement age account in part for a projected decline in the Social Security replacement rate (Table 3.7).

## Savings Estimate

Life-expectancy indexing of U.S. Social Security benefits would be a major step toward resolving the program's future financial problems. The Congressional Budget Office (CBO) has estimated the effect of a reform that involved life-expectancy indexing of initial Social Security benefits. This one change, put into effect in 2012, would eliminate 43 percent of Social Security's 75-year deficit and would push back the date of insolvency by seven years (CBO 2005). An alternative estimate has indicated a smaller effect, with 27 percent of the deficit eliminated (Shelton 2008).

The two estimates differ in part because of the different ways that life-expectancy indexing is applied. The CBO estimate adjusts for the percentage change in life expectancy at age 65, while the Shelton estimate adjusts for the percentage change in the present value of lifetime benefits due to the increase in life expectancy.[9] An alternative estimate indicates that life-expectancy indexing of initial benefits at retirement

**Table 3.7  United States: Changes in Contributions and Benefits**

| System parameter | Value (%) |
|---|---|
| Contributions: employer-employee tax rate | |
|   Rate in 2008 | 12.4 |
|   Future rate | 12.4 |
| Benefits: replacement rate (avg. worker) | |
|   Rate in 2008 | 41.0 |
|   Future rate (2030) | 37.0 |

NOTE: The replacement rate is projected to fall for three reasons: 1) the increase in the normal retirement age, which acts as a cut in benefits; 2) an increased share of benefits being taxable; and 3) increased contributions for Medicare, which are deducted from Social Security benefits.
SOURCE: Munnell (2003).

by correcting for the change in the present value of benefits would reduce the Social Security benefits of new retirees by about 0.24 percent per year (Goss 2003).

## Growth Rate of Benefits

In the U.S. Social Security system, initial benefits at retirement are designed to grow with the growth rate of average real wages in the economy. The system achieves that result by indexing Social Security–covered wages to age 60 by the growth rate of average wages.[10]

A number of countries have reformed their systems to slow the growth rate in average benefits to below the growth rate of average wages, which is the growth measure used in the U.S. Social Security system. In Sweden, initial benefits at retirement grow at the growth rate of average wages minus an adjustment for the increase in life expectancy. In Japan, the average benefit level grows at the growth rate of average wages less the growth rate in life expectancy.

The policies of one country may work differently when applied in another country. For example, countries differ in their degree of income inequality and degree of population heterogeneity with respect to life expectancy. For example, Sweden may have greater toleration than the United States for cutting the real value of social security benefits in payment because it has a low poverty rate for older persons. Using internationally comparative data, in Sweden 2.1 percent of the population aged 65 and older has income below 40 percent of the median income, compared with 15.0 percent in the United States (Luxembourg Income Study 2007).

## CONCLUSIONS

Increasingly, countries are adopting automatic adjustment mechanisms for social security financing. These mechanisms attempt to deal with problems of sustainability and of political risk. While political risk has been reduced by these changes, it remains in most systems because of oversight of the process by the government and the potential need for further reforms due to declining replacement rates.

Countries have relatively little experience with life-expectancy indexing of benefits, so it is not possible yet to assess the long-term effects of such policies. Countries may eventually decide that life-expectancy indexing of benefits results in too large a drop in the replacement rate. That said, the drop can be offset by workers who choose to work longer or by a policy encouraging longer work years, for example by raising the social security eligibility age.

As of 2010, only one country—Denmark—has indexed the social security eligibility age. The United Kingdom considered such a proposal but adopted quasi indexing instead, a method in which the age rises according to a fixed schedule.

Automatic indexing done annually involves regular, incremental changes. This type of indexing becomes part of the regular functioning of the social security system. However, for indexing to function as it is designed, it must be supported by a broad-based political commitment not to seek vote-winning modifications that undermine its effectiveness. In this regard, it might appear likely that the automatic adjustment mechanisms would work in Sweden and Japan because of the consensus nature of their politics. Sweden, however, revised its automatic adjustment mechanism to modify its effects. Italy and Germany have also overridden automatic adjustments. Thus, the international experience does not provide a clear lesson as to how this type of adjustment would work in the United States.

## POLICY RECOMMENDATIONS

This chapter recommends that an automatic adjustment mechanism be adopted to help restore and maintain Social Security's solvency. It recommends that Social Security benefits be indexed for life expectancy, so that increases in life expectancy would not cause an increase in the lifetime value of pension benefits. This type of indexation has been adopted by Sweden for its social security program. With this type of indexation, every year for each new retirement cohort, there would be a slight downward adjustment in benefits to take into account the effect of increased life expectancy on the lifetime value of benefits. The adjustment would occur for each cohort only once, with benefits received at retirement facing no further adjustments. This type of indexation results in a reduced replacement rate over time. The following two chapters consider policies that address that issue.

# Notes

1. This chapter is largely based on Turner (2009).
2. The projection for life expectancy at age 60 in 2012 is 21.8 years, which is 54.5 percent of the 40-year working period starting at age 20 (Whitehouse 2007a).
3. This aspect of the Swedish system is similar to the U.S. Social Security system, where benefits are indexed to the growth rate in average wages. However, a difference is that the U.S. system can increase tax rates without having that change raise benefit entitlements, which the Swedish system cannot do.
4. The actual procedure for calculating the present value of future contributions is somewhat different. The expected turnover distribution is calculated as the difference between the expected average pension–weighted age of benefit receipt, which is 76, and the expected average income–weighted age of payroll tax payments, which is 43. The difference between those two ages is 33. Total assets are measured as the buffer fund plus 33 times annual contributions.
5. The NDC system has few actual assets because it is funded on a pay-as-you-go basis with a reserve fund that is small relative to liabilities. To calculate assets for the purposes of the automatic balancing mechanism, the annual contributions received by the system are multiplied by what is called the expected turnover duration. The expected turnover duration is the average length of time, measured in years, until the system must pay out benefits to liquidate the liability created in the current year. It can be shown that if the population structure of the system is stationary, the present value of benefits accrued during a year equals the contributions during the year times the turnover duration. (Japan has evaluated this method of determining the future liabilities of its system and decided that it would not work for the country because it has a declining workforce rather than a stable population structure [Sakamoto 2005].)

    This value of assets is compared to the present value at the end of the fiscal year of the liabilities for future benefit payments. If assets exceed or equal liabilities in value, no adjustment is made. If assets are less than liabilities, the rate of return credited to the notional account balances is reduced, and the indexing of current benefits is reduced. To smooth out temporary variations, the calculation is done on the basis of a three-year moving average of the ratio of assets to liabilities (Könberg, Palmer, and Sundén 2006). Similar to the U.S. Social Security system, Sweden's system calculates three projections: 1) a base case, 2) an optimistic case, and 3) a pessimistic case. It uses the base case for determining whether an adjustment is needed and the other two cases for determining the range of possible future outcomes.

6. Balancing affects the NDC benefit. Beneficiaries without income-related benefits or with low NDC benefits can qualify for the minimum guarantee government benefit. Among Sweden's 1.8 million retirees, approximately 800,000 have some guarantee benefit. When the NDC benefit is reduced, guarantee benefits will increase for beneficiaries with both benefits. Thus, the net effect on total benefits will be less for this group.

7. With the sustainability factor $A$, the benefit formula is multiplied by the following factor:

$$A = 1 + \alpha(1 - R),$$

where $R$ is the ratio of the dependency rate in year $t - 2$ (i.e., two years earlier) to the dependency rate in year $t - 3$, and is thus a number greater than 1 because of the increasing dependency ratio over time. The parameter $\alpha$ has been set in the German reform at 0.25. If it had been set at zero, there would be no sustainability factor adjustment. If it had been set at one, the impact of changes in the dependency rate would fall entirely on benefits, with no increase in the payroll tax rate. It was set at 0.25 because that adjustment factor would result in future payroll taxes rising to no more than 20 percent in 2020 and 22 percent in 2030, based on current projections (Toft 2007). The term $\alpha(1 - R)$ (where $\alpha$ is greater than zero) is negative (but greater than $-1$), making the sustainability factor $A$ have a positive value that is less than 1.

An example clarifies how this operates. If the dependency rate is growing at 2 percent a year, which is more rapidly than the U.S. dependency rate is projected to grow between 2000 and 2030 (Table 3.1), $R$ would equal 1.02, $\alpha(1 - R)$ would equal $-0.005$, and $A$ would equal 0.995. This means that benefits would grow at 0.5 percent less than the growth rate of average wages.

8. Japan decided not to follow the Swedish approach, which involves calculating the turnover ratio, because in the context of the Japanese social security system it is difficult to calculate that measure. This difficulty arises because of the variety of types of linked benefits, including disability benefits, provided by the Japanese system.

9. The difference may also be explained in part by the differences in the underlying models for calculating Social Security's financing: the CBO model calculates a smaller long-term deficit than the approach used by the Social Security Administration actuaries.

10. Once in payment, benefits are indexed to prices.

# 4

# Raising the Early Retirement Age

Even if Social Security were not projected to have insufficient funds based on current life expectancy, continued increases in life expectancy would cause an insufficiency to occur in the future. Therefore, a practical reform proposal to maintain Social Security's solvency should include an adjustment of Social Security for rising longevity.

Many policy options could deal with the effects of increasing life expectancy on Social Security financing.[1] First, the normal retirement age could be raised to a higher predetermined age. In the 1983 amendments to the Social Security Act, the normal retirement age was raised from 65 to 67, and that change is being phased in with a long delay, only taking full effect for people born in 1960 or later. The normal retirement age is also referred to as the full retirement age, but neither term is descriptively accurate. It is the age at which a worker can receive Social Security benefits that are not reduced for early retirement. It varies from age 65 to 67, based on year of birth. For example, for workers born between 1943 and 1954, the normal retirement age is 66. Liebman, MacGuineas, and Samwick (2005) suggest that the normal retirement age be raised to 68.

Second, the normal retirement age could be indexed to rise as the life expectancy of retirees increases. The 1994–1996 Advisory Council on Social Security included such a measure in its recommendations.[2] Third, the normal retirement age could remain fixed, with benefits indexed to life expectancy, so that benefits gradually decline as longevity rises for successive cohorts, as recommended in Chapter 3. Fourth, the early retirement age could be raised, with the benefits currently receivable at age 62 being received at age 63. Other options include raising the payroll tax rate, raising the payroll tax ceiling, adding general revenue funding, changing the benefit formula, and changing the number of years used in calculating Social Security benefits.

While raising the early retirement age is not a popular idea, none of the options for restoring solvency pass that test. For more than 40 years, Social Security's early retirement age of 62 has been an important benchmark for workers considering retiring. Raising it to keep it in line with increases in life expectancy could have a powerful effect on the retirement decisions of workers and on all retirement program costs, in both the public and private sectors. To allow workers ample time to adjust their plans, if the eligibility age for Social Security were raised to 63, such a change would presumably occur with a long delay, possibly 20 years, and with a phase-in period.[3]

An early retirement age of 63 has international precedents. In Germany, for example, the early retirement age is 63, while in the United Kingdom it is currently 65 for men, and is being raised over time to 65 for women. In Switzerland it is 65 for men and 63 for women. In New Zealand and Ireland, it is 65 (Turner 2007).

In addition, historical precedent supports a higher early retirement age. In 1940, when Social Security first paid benefits, the earliest age at which workers could receive benefits was even higher—age 65. For more than 20 years, the earliest age at which men could receive Social Security benefits remained at 65. In 1961, the early retirement age for men was reduced to 62. The reduction for women had occurred five years earlier, in 1956.

Chapter 2 considered issues relating to whether older workers would generally be able to extend their work lives if the early retirement age for Social Security were raised. Evidence presented in that chapter indicates that life expectancy has increased for both men and women, and for all major demographic groups in the United States. In addition, the physical demands of work have decreased, though not for everyone.

This chapter considers a possible policy change of raising the early retirement age in Social Security from age 62 to 63 as one step toward dealing with increased longevity. Arguably, this change would be superior to the alternative of workers receiving less in Social Security benefits in the future. Either this change could be done in an ad hoc way, or it could be done through life-expectancy indexing, as discussed in the previous chapter. This chapter surveys early eligibility ages and eligibility requirements for social security old-age benefits in other OECD countries, plus selected other countries with informative experience. A focus of the chapter is on the attempts of various countries to provide flexible early eligibility requirements that are targeted to meet the needs of groups with particular characteristics as to their work histories. At the end of the chapter, an alternative to raising the early retirement age is considered, which is a flexible full retirement age that varies by income level (Monk, Turner, and Zhivan 2010).

## VIEWS ON RAISING THE EARLY RETIREMENT AGE

It is important to distinguish between changes in lifetime Social Security benefits and changes in annual benefits. Changes in lifetime benefits affect the wealth value of Social Security and measures of its money's worth. Changes in annual benefits more directly relate to measures of the adequacy of Social Security, such as the replacement rate. These changes can be viewed from different perspectives.

No changes in the Social Security program, including no changes in annual benefits, would mean that lifetime benefits would increase over time because of the increase in life expectancy. This change occurs both for high-income workers and low-income workers, because life expectancy has increased over time for both groups. Both annual benefits and lifetime benefits could be maintained if the Social Security early retirement age were increased over time to offset the effect of increases in life expectancy on lifetime benefits. Such a change would not adversely affect either high-income or low-income workers if it were done by adjusting for the lesser improvement in life expectancy experienced by low-income workers.

It is often argued that raising the early retirement age is adverse to low-income workers. They have a shorter life expectancy than high-income workers, and thus an increase in the early retirement age constitutes a greater percentage decline in their years of retirement than it does for high-income workers. This argument views the change at a point in time, rather than in the broader framework that includes considering changes in life expectancy over time. Economists have generally moved from point-in-time analyses of issues affecting workers to life-cycle analyses.

Under a life-cycle analysis, a worker is promised a pension benefit when the worker begins work—say, at age 22. When the worker retires more than 40 years later, the value of the promised benefit has increased considerably for defined benefit plans because of the increase in life expectancy that has occurred over that period. Raising the early retirement age to take that increase in life expectancy into account would not constitute a reduction in lifetime benefits, but would merely offset the increase in payment that was due to rising life expectancy over the period.

Raising the early retirement age could be motivated by a desire to reduce Social Security's benefit costs. Lifetime benefits would effectively be cut if the reform resulted in age 62 benefits being receivable at age 63. For workers born in 1960 and later, those who retire at age 62 would receive an amount equal to 70 percent of their Primary Insurance Amount (PIA), which is the unreduced value of Social Security benefits if they are received at the normal retirement age, which is 67 for these workers. Those retiring at age 63 would receive 75 percent of their PIA. Thus, workers retiring at age 62 would receive the same level of annual benefits but one fewer year of benefits. Workers retiring at age 63 and later would receive lower benefits. For those retiring at 63, the benefits would be 9.3 percent lower (70/75).

However, another motivation for raising the early retirement age might be to raise annual benefit levels to offset other benefit cuts. The annual benefits of persons taking retirement at age 62 could be raised by raising the early retirement age to 63, with no reduction in annual benefits receivable at that age. In this case, workers formerly retiring at age 62 would receive one fewer year of benefits, but they would gain from the postponement in benefit receipt and consequently would receive benefits that were 7.1 percent higher (75/70). Those retiring at age 63 or later would have no change in their benefits.

Workers could voluntarily postpone the age at which they take Social Security benefits past age 62, and many do. Social Security is roughly actuarially fair at age 62, so that for a person with life expectancy equal to the actuarially assumed life expectancy, expected lifetime benefits at age 62 are the same as at age 63 for a person delaying receipt of benefits. For a person who not only delayed receiving benefits but also continued working, generally their benefits would be higher because of the continued work.

Since the option of postponing receipt of benefits to age 63 is already available, the question arises as to why that option should be made mandatory. First, because they have financial myopia, some workers opt to receive benefits at age 62, not taking into account that they might be better off over the remainder of their lifetime by receiving higher benefits but at a later age. Second, the incentive to postpone retirement built into the Social Security benefit structure only operates for people with relatively long life expectancy. For persons with life expectancy shorter than average, their incentive in terms of maximizing lifetime benefits is to retire at age 62. Third, while some people are poor planners because of myopia, persons wishing to leave the labor force at age 62 still are free to do so, especially if they plan so that they finance their retirement at that age through additional savings from other sources.

## COMPARABLE EARLY RETIREMENT AGES WITH INCREASES IN LIFE EXPECTANCY

With increases in life expectancy and improvements in health at older ages, a case can be made that the early retirement age should also increase. From a life-cycle perspective, rather than assuming a one-for-one increase in retirement age with an increase in life expectancy, a rule of thumb would be to maintain a constant proportion of life spent in retirement. The life-cycle perspective would consider the balance between the years working (and saving for retirement) compared to the years retired because of the focus on financing retirement years with working years.

Assuming that the number of years in retirement is roughly 20, and that someone who has worked a full career has worked roughly 40 years, then the number of years in retirement is half the number of years spent working. In that case, the early retirement age would be raised by two-thirds of the increase in life expectancy to maintain a constant ratio of retirement years to working years.

Table 4.1 shows the increases in life expectancy by race and gender since 1950 and 1960. It makes various calculations of what might be considered a comparable early retirement age. At the high end, if workers had the same number of years of life remaining in 2006 as they did in 1950, when the early retirement age was 65, the early retirement age could be raised to 67 and each race-gender group would still be better off than the earlier generation by one year. Taking the life-cycle perspective of maintaining the same ratio of retirement years to work-

**Table 4.1  Comparable Early Retirement Ages with an Increase in Life Expectancy at Age 65, by Race and Sex, 1950–2006 (years)**

| Year | White men | White women | Black men | Black women |
|---|---|---|---|---|
| 1950 | 12.8 | 15.1 | 12.9 | 14.9 |
| 1960 | 12.9 | 15.9 | 12.7 | 15.1 |
| 2006 | 17.1 | 19.8 | 15.1 | 18.6 |
| Change in life expectancy from 1950 (from 1960) | 4.3 (4.2) | 4.7 (3.9) | 2.2 (2.4) | 3.7 (3.5) |
| Comparable early retirement age to 1950 (age 65) in 2003 in terms of number of years in retirement | 69.3 | 69.7 | 67.2 | 68.7 |
| Comparable early retirement age to 1961 (age 62) in 2003 in terms of number of years in retirement | 66.2 | 65.9 | 64.4 | 65.5 |
| Comparable early retirement age to 1961 (age 62) in 2003 assuming retirement years are one-half of work years | 64.8 | 64.6 | 63.6 | 64.3 |

SOURCE: National Center for Health Statistics (2009b) and author's calculations.

ing years and comparing to 1961 (using data for 1960), when the early retirement age was 62, the early retirement age could be raised to 63, with each race-gender group being better off than the earlier generation.

## FAIRNESS

Fairness is an important aspect of the issue of raising Social Security's early retirement age. Would such a change be fair to demographic groups with relatively short life expectancy, to people with physically demanding jobs, or to people at older ages unable to work or to find work? The issue of fairness can be addressed in terms of either cross-sectional equity or intergenerational equity. To examine cross-sectional equity, we compare workers at different income levels at a point in time. However, because workers worked to older ages early in the history of Social Security, the past becomes a natural point of comparison, which is a comparison of intergenerational equity.

Munnell et al. (2004) note that raising the early retirement age without any associated cut in benefits would result in greater lifetime Social Security wealth (the expected present value of Social Security benefits) for long-lived demographic groups and less Social Security wealth for short-lived groups. By this measure, such a policy is relatively advantageous to women and disadvantageous to blacks because of their relatively longer and shorter life expectancies. This measure considers equity across a generation.

Addressing the issue of cross-sectional equity, a simulation study has examined the distributional effects on people of raising the Social Security early retirement age from 62 to 65 (Mermin and Steuerle 2006). That study finds that workers in all income quintiles would receive lower lifetime Social Security benefits. However, workers in the lowest income quintile are least affected as a group, in part because a higher percentage of them receive Social Security disability benefits. In that simulation, it was assumed that the level of benefits and age at first receipt for Social Security disability benefits would not be affected by raising the Social Security early retirement age.

Using intergenerational equity as a measure of fairness, different demographic groups are compared to their counterparts in earlier generations. By the intergenerational method, all groups, including blacks and women, are relatively better able to work at older ages, and would still be able to spend a higher percentage of their adult life in retirement, if the early retirement age were raised. Thus, it can be argued that raising the early retirement age would violate neither standards of cross-sectional equity nor intergenerational equity.


## AN ALTERNATIVE TO BENEFIT CUTS


If the projected future insolvency of Social Security is dealt with through benefit cuts, eventually the replacement rate provided at the early retirement age would fall to where it would be viewed as unacceptably low. The replacement rate provided by Social Security is already not generous by international standards. With changes in law that already have been legislated, average earners retiring at age 62 will see their replacement rate fall from 30 percent today to 23 percent in 2030. These replacement rates are net of Medicare part B premiums, but they do not include possible future benefit cuts made to restore Social Security's solvency (Munnell et al. 2004).

If benefits were cut to restore solvency, a cut in benefits for people retiring at 62 could be offset by raising the early retirement age. More than half of workers eligible to claim Social Security benefits do so at 62, the early retirement age in Social Security (Panis et al. 2002).[4] If benefits were cut by 7 percent but the early retirement age was raised by one year, from 62 to 63, people retiring at age 63 instead of 62 would receive roughly the same level of annual benefits as before the cut, thus helping to maintain Social Security's ability to keep people out of poverty and to provide a base level of retirement income. If people worked the extra year, their annual benefits would generally be higher than before the benefit cut because of their extra work and postponed retirement.

Raising the early retirement age from 62 to 63 would raise the annual benefits of those claiming before age 63 because of the actuarial adjustment for postponed benefit receipt. It could further raise their benefits if these claimants worked the additional year. People already claiming Social Security benefits at age 63 or later would be unaffected by this change, since the benefits receivable at age 63 and higher would be unaffected. The effect on Social Security solvency of raising the early retirement age would be negligible because on average, across the population, raising this age does not affect the expected lifetime level of benefits. However, without changes in other programs targeted to help vulnerable older workers, such a change might significantly reduce the level of lifetime benefits for individuals who are forced to claim early because of poor health or poor labor market opportunities (Zhivan et al. 2008).

## INTERNATIONAL EXPERIENCE

The international experience across the OECD countries varies considerably concerning age and eligibility requirements for early retirement under Social Security. Most U.S. workers are able to qualify for benefits at the early retirement age of 62, but for some countries, eligibility requirements are designed to permit long-career workers—who started work at relatively young ages and who also tend to be less educated—to receive old-age benefits at earlier ages than others. The eligibility requirements are based on an attempt to permit people who may be less able to continue work at older ages, but who do not qualify for disability benefits, to retire relatively early.

In the international context, pensionable age may be a preferable term to early retirement age because for some countries the earliest age is 65 or even higher. A pensionable age of 65 is becoming increasingly common in OECD countries. In 1993, nearly half of the 23 OECD countries (11) had a pensionable age of 65 or higher for men (Turner 2007). By 2035, three-fifths of the countries (14) are scheduled to have a pensionable age of 65 or higher, based on current legislation. However, looking backwards, four-fifths of the countries (19) had a pensionable age of at least 65 in 1949. Thus, both historical precedent and current legislation support the feasibility of a pensionable age of 65—three years higher than the U.S. age of 62.

In 2002, in about a third of the traditional OECD countries (7), the pensionable age was lower for workers with 40 years of work than for those with 30 years of work (Turner 2007). In a few countries (3), the pensionable age was higher for workers with 10 years of work than for those with 30 years of work; in addition, in a few countries (3), workers were ineligible for old-age benefits with only 10 years of work.

Related policies designed to encourage postponed work include

- raising the qualifying conditions for eligibility for benefits at the pensionable age,
- reducing the level of benefits available at the pensionable age,
- raising the incentive for postponing retirement by increasing the amount by which benefits are raised with delayed retirement, and

- reducing the availability of alternative pathways to early retirement.

## Countries That Have Raised the Early Retirement Age

While many U.S. policy analysts consider it to be politically difficult to raise the early retirement age for Social Security, since the early 1990s a number of countries have done so, motivated by the desire to reduce budgetary outlays and encourage postponed retirement.

In describing the legislated changes, we give attention to aspects of the timing of the increase—the length of the initial delay after the legislation was enacted until the first increase, and the length of the phase-in or transition period. The following examples identify selected countries that have raised the pensionable age for both men and women.

- In 2002, Finland legislated changes that took effect in 2005. The pensionable age in the social security earnings-related pension system was raised from 60 to 62, and the individual early retirement pension, which had been available at age 58 to long-service workers, was abolished (OECD 2008).

- Greece raised the pensionable age to 65 for both men and women who began working after 1993 and who have had short- or medium-length working careers. The current pensionable age, however, is 58 for men and women with long careers (10,500 days, or approximately 40 years) and age 60 for men and women with 4,500 days (approximately 18 years) of contributions.

- Japan is raising the pensionable age for both its flat rate social security pension (National Pension) and its earnings-related pension (Employees' Pension Insurance Scheme). Legislation Japan passed in 1995 raised the pensionable age for its flat rate pension by one year every three years; it will reach 65 in 2014. For sailors and miners, because of the physical difficulty of their work, the pensionable age for the flat rate pension will not reach 65 until 2030. Based on legislation passed in 2000, Japan is raising the pensionable age for its earnings-related pension (Employees' Pension Insurance) by one year every three years starting in 2013. With these changes, men born after 1960 and

women born after 1965 have a pensionable age for both programs of 65.

- New Zealand raised its pensionable age from 60 in 1991 to 65
  in 2001. Those workers who turned 60 before March 31, 1992,
  were eligible for a social security benefit at age 60. The legislation passed August 1, 1991, and took effect the following April
  1, when eligibility increased from age 60 to 61. Beginning July
  1, 1993, eligibility rose by three months for each six-month period until April 1, 2001, when the pensionable age reached 65.
  Thus, a five-year increase in the pensionable age was phased
  in over nine years. A Transitional Retirement Benefit was paid
  over this period to those affected by the changes, and the age of
  eligibility for this benefit also rose, until it was phased out on
  April 1, 2001.

Some OECD countries have had a long-standing pensionable age
of 65. In Australia, Austria, Germany, Switzerland, and the United
Kingdom, the pensionable age for men has been 65 since at least 1949.
In Ireland, the social security retirement pension is available at age 65
for both men and women.

## Countries That Have Restricted Qualifying Conditions

Some countries have increased the incentive for postponed retirement by raising the amount by which benefits increase when a worker
delays retirement. The United States has done that for retirement postponed beyond the normal retirement age up to age 70. The United
States has also eliminated the earnings test for working Social Security
beneficiaries older than the normal retirement age (currently age 66).
Some countries, including the United States, have attempted to reduce
the effect of their social security pensionable age on retirement ages by
moving toward actuarial neutrality concerning the effect of postponed
retirement on the present value of social security benefits. That change,
however, only makes Social Security neutral for people with roughly
the average life expectancy, but still leaves incentive effects for people
with significantly longer or shorter life expectancies.

## Countries That Have Restricted the Availability of Pathways That Facilitate a Relatively High Pensionable Age

Countries with a relatively high pensionable age usually establish policies for people unable to work at older ages that provide alternative pathways to retirement. The effective retirement age in countries with a relatively high pensionable age is generally at least several years lower than the pensionable age in social security, due in part to alternative exit routes from the labor force. The easy availability of disability insurance and unemployment insurance benefits for older workers facilitates early retirement in some countries, since these programs serve as de facto early retirement programs. Because of alternative pathways to early retirement, in many countries the pensionable age has a limited effect on retirement ages. However, that situation is changing as some countries restrict the availability of alternative pathways to early retirement.

In Australia, a pensionable age of 65 is facilitated by having a two-tiered mandatory old-age benefit, with one tier having a lower pensionable age. The pensionable age for the means-tested old-age benefit (the age pension) is 65 for men and will rise to 65 for women by 2013. Workers can receive the mandatory employer-provided benefit at age 55; this is being raised to age 60.

A pensionable age of 65 or higher is facilitated as a social policy in some countries, such as Germany, by having a lower pensionable age for long-service workers. This policy allows workers who have had long careers to retire early. This type of policy may help workers with long years of work in physically demanding jobs. It often, however, does not help women because they traditionally have interrupted their work in the labor market to care for children, though some countries give limited credit for child rearing.

Some countries offer government-provided early retirement benefits through a separate program. In Denmark, workers can receive the state-sponsored early retirement benefit at age 60. In Iceland, workers can receive their mandatory occupational pension benefits in their two-tier system at age 62 (OECD 2008). Also, many older workers receive disability benefits. In Norway, nearly all workers are covered by a generous early retirement pension that provides benefits at age 62. The early retirement pension is considered to be a private sector pension, but the government pays 40 percent of the cost.

In the United Kingdom, workers who contract out of (withdraw from) the social security benefit can receive their contracted-out private sector benefit at a younger age, as specified by the rules for their plan, than they could receive their state benefit, or at age 60 if they contract out using an individual account (personal pension).

In the Netherlands, the basic social security old-age pension is available at age 65; however, the country's early retirement program (VUT), developed in the early 1980s, provides an alternative exit from the workforce. With at least 10 years of uninterrupted employment, a worker aged 60 can retire with a replacement rate of at least 80 percent. The government in 2003 announced plans to phase out this system (Brooksbank 2003), and in 2004 legislation was passed ending the tax subsidy for the VUT except for people aged 55 or older on January 1, 2005 (Rossingh 2004). It has also ended the tax deductibility of long-term sickness and early retirement pensions.

In addition, some countries have a lower pensionable age for workers in certain arduous occupations, such as mining and fishing. Greece, Japan, Portugal, and Spain are examples.

## FLEXIBLE NORMAL RETIREMENT AGE

Increasing the normal retirement age in the United States while holding the early retirement age fixed could be effective in reducing Social Security program costs, but eventually it will result in replacement rates that are viewed by many as too low. A possible policy to maintain replacement rates is to raise the early retirement age. However, an increase in the early retirement age introduces possible unfairness because the variation in life expectancy across socioeconomic groups is positively correlated with lifetime income. A flexible normal retirement age is an alternative policy that could preserve or even enhance the progressivity of Social Security benefits. If life expectancy were correlated with lifetime income, Social Security policy could use the AIME (Average Indexed Monthly Earnings) to target policies that are more equitable for people with both lower lifetime income and lower life expectancy. However, while life expectancy is strongly correlated with AIME for men, it is only weakly correlated for women, and when pooling the genders the correlation disappears (Monk, Turner, and Zhivan 2010). Alternatively, targeting could be done by the "max AIME," which is the AIME for single persons and the maximum of the husband's or wife's AIME for married couples. Monk, Turner, and Zhivan find that the max AIME, which is a household measure of lifetime income, could be used for constructing a flexible normal retirement age because it is negatively correlated with mortality risk and also negatively correlated with other measures of economic vulnerability or inability to work at older ages. With a flexible normal retirement age, individuals in households with a low max AIME would have a lower normal retirement age than other individuals.

## RAISING THE MAXIMUM AGE FOR ACTUARIAL ADJUSTMENT OF BENEFITS

If the early retirement age is raised, the same arguments justifying that change should also lead to an increase in the maximum age for actuarial increases in benefits. This change would benefit people who continue working into older ages, but also would encourage people to do so. Currently, the Social Security Administration adjusts benefits for postponement of receipt up to age 70 in the United States. If the early retirement age is increased to age 63, the maximum age for actuarial adjustment should be raised in tandem to 71.

## POLICY RECOMMENDATIONS

This book recommends that the early retirement age in Social Security be raised to age 63, with that change being phased in starting in 15 years, and that thereafter it be periodically adjusted to take into account continuing improvements in life expectancy. The initial change would occur at the rate of 2 months every other year, so that for persons aged 47 the new early retirement age would be 62 years and 2 months; for persons aged 45, it would be 62 years and 4 months; and so on.

If this change were done to help restore solvency, the benefits receivable at the new early retirement age would be the same as those currently receivable at age 62. This change would both encourage postponed retirement and address Social Security's financing. Alternatively, if this change were done in conjunction with the recommended life-expectancy indexing of benefits, proposed in Chapter Three, the benefits receivable at age 63 would be the same as those receivable at 63 before the increase in the early retirement age.

If Congress raises the early retirement age, then the same arguments justifying that change should also lead it to raise the maximum age for actuarial increases in benefits. Currently, benefits are adjusted for postponement of receipt up to age 70. If Congress should raise the early retirement age to 63, then it should also increase the maximum age for actuarial adjustment to 71.

## Notes

1. See Social Security Advisory Board (2005) for a discussion of various additional options. In addition, see Turner (2009) for an international comparison of longevity-related reforms to social security systems.
2. The Advisory Council's report is available at http://www.ssa.gov/history/reports/ adcouncil/report/toc.htm (accessed January 5, 2011). The American Academy of Actuaries also advocates indexing the normal retirement age to longevity.
3. See Turner (2007) for international experience with such a policy.
4. This is also referred to by different authors as the early entitlement age, the early eligibility age, and the pensionable age.

# 5
# Longevity Insurance Benefits

With increased longevity, retirees face an increased risk of having insufficient resources to maintain their standard of living at older ages. While Social Security provides a guaranteed lifetime benefit, that benefit is insufficient for most retirees to maintain their preretirement standard of living. Thus, most people need to supplement their Social Security benefits with other sources of income. While the causes of old-age poverty are complex, one factor is that as people grow older, especially if they live longer than they expected to, they risk exhausting their sources of income other than Social Security. People in their eighties with low Social Security benefits are particularly economically vulnerable. Few are able to compensate for a loss of non–Social Security income by working. People in this age group, often called the old-old, may not have sufficient resources to enjoy the last years of their lives without financial worries.

This chapter proposes a new type of Social Security benefit, called longevity insurance, which may be particularly useful for this vulnerable group. This proposed benefit strengthens social insurance for people in their eighties and older by adding longevity insurance to the social insurance protection Social Security provides. Longevity insurance is a deferred annuity that starts at an advanced age. Much of the utility value to workers of annuitization is provided by this benefit because the annuity value comes from insuring against the possibility of running resources down to a very low level if one lives to be older than expected (Brown 2001). The benefit would be supplied through Social Security and would be universally available, but with eligibility based on a benefits test, so that only people with low Social Security benefits would receive it.

The longevity insurance benefit proposed here is an enhanced Social Security benefit starting at age 82, which is roughly the life expectancy of someone retiring at age 62. Qualifying persons receiving a Social Security benefit below a minimum level would have their benefit raised at that age.

Longevity insurance can be an important component of a policy package to restore Social Security solvency. Public policy changes to restore solvency likely will reduce the generosity of Social Security old-age benefits as part of a package of changes. Most reform packages that cut benefits would raise elderly poverty. To offset that effect, policymakers may want to increase the generosity of some benefits to better target benefits to vulnerable groups. That goal could be achieved by providing longevity insurance benefits. This insurance shifts Social Security resources toward persons who both are old and have low incomes, and thus provides better targeting of limited resources in terms of the protection provided to vulnerable persons.

## AN INCREASING RISK OF POVERTY WITH ADVANCING AGE

Poverty rates among older persons increase with age. Elderly poverty is especially high among people aged 80 and older—a third higher than for people aged 65–69 (Whitman and Purcell 2006). Poverty is particularly a problem for older women (Smith 2003). Women aged 80 and older had a poverty rate of 14 percent in 2004, and 25 percent had income below 125 percent of the poverty line, compared to 10 percent and 13 percent for women aged 55 to 61 (Social Security Administration 2006). A reason for the increase in poverty at older ages is a decline in the importance of non–Social Security sources of retirement income at older ages.

Official poverty statistics understate the problem of poverty in this age group because they no longer represent the minimum needs of older persons. They are based on a methodology established in 1964. For that reason, 125 percent of poverty is often used as a better measure of persons with insufficient resources (Butrica and Zedlewski 2008). However, even that figure understates the percentage of older women who have fallen into poverty. If no one fell into poverty as they aged, poverty rates would decline at older ages because of the greater mortality risk of low-income persons as compared to high-income persons.

## Risks Leading to Poverty in Old Age

People over the age of 80 are at risk of falling into poverty even if they have not been poor earlier in life. Also, they have greater difficulty leaving poverty than people at younger ages (Lee and Shaw 2008). The problem of poverty at advanced ages may be growing over time because while the bankruptcy rate for persons under age 55 fell during the period from 1991 to 2007, it more than quadrupled for people aged 75 to 84 (Sedensky 2008).

Except for Social Security, most people do not receive retirement income in the form of a price-indexed annuity. Partially for that reason, people who were not already in poverty can fall into poverty at older ages. This may particularly be a problem during periods of increasing longevity, if people underestimate how long they will live and they fail to plan adequately for a longer retirement.

The MetLife Retirement Income IQ Study (MetLife Mature Market Institute 2008) provides evidence as to errors in retirement planning that make a longevity insurance benefit desirable. It finds that nearly 70 percent of preretirees overestimate how much they can withdraw from their savings and assure that their savings will last. More than 40 percent indicate that they think they can withdraw 10 percent of their savings each year while preserving their principal, while 14 percent believe they can draw down 15 percent per year while maintaining their principal. Almost half estimate that they will need 50 percent or less of their preretirement income to maintain their consumption in retirement, while financial planners tend to put the figure in the range of 70 to 80 percent, depending on family circumstances, such as number of children. Six in ten underestimate their chances of living beyond average life expectancy.

While the causes of old-age poverty are complex, in part because of these problems in planning for retirement income at older ages, a leading cause is that a higher percentage of people at advanced older ages depend on Social Security for most or all of their income than do people in their sixties and early seventies. For households aged 75 and older, 40 percent depend on Social Security for 90 percent or more of their income, compared to 27 percent of people aged 65 to 74 (Social Security Administration 2006).

## LONGEVITY INSURANCE

Longevity insurance is a special type of annuity. Annuities are financial instruments that pay a stream of benefits over time. A life annuity pays fixed nominal benefits periodically until death. Annuities can be purchased privately or through pension plans. Social Security benefits are also an annuity. Workers can purchase an immediate annuity at retirement, or they can purchase a deferred annuity for receipt at a later age.

Longevity insurance is a deferred annuity that starts at an advanced age, such as 82. It is less commonly called an advanced life deferred annuity. While all annuities provide a degree of longevity insurance, in recent years that term has been used to refer to a deferred annuity starting payment at an advanced age. Adding longevity insurance to Social Security would address the problem of people falling into poverty at advanced ages, and it would provide cost-effective social insurance.

This insurance protection is similar to buying car or home insurance with a large deductible, which optimally deals with catastrophic risk. Longevity insurance provides insurance against outliving one's assets, but only when that risk becomes substantial at advanced ages (Milevsky 2005). Making assumptions about risk aversion (a coefficient of risk aversion of five), one study calculates that a longevity insurance annuity beginning at age 85 provides 62 percent of the longevity insurance of an annuity beginning at age 60 (Webb, Gong, and Sun 2007). In actual practice, a longevity insurance annuity would probably be sold at more of an actuarially unfair price than a regular annuity because of the greater presumption of longer-than-average life expectancy.

The life cycle theory suggests that rational planners may not save for a level of consumption at advanced ages that is equivalent to the consumption at earlier ages because of the low probability of being alive at advanced ages. A longevity insurance annuity allows a person, at low cost relative to the benefit received, to obtain an annuity that only pays benefits at advanced ages (Webb, Gong, and Sun 2007). An advantage of this type of annuity for life cycle planning is that workers may be able to consume more of their nonannuitized resources in their sixties and seventies, knowing that they have longevity insurance that protects them if they live longer than their life expectancy.

Annuity benefits can conceptually be divided into two components: old-age benefits and longevity insurance benefits. Longevity insurance benefits are a hedge against life expectancy risk. Increases in life expectancy at retirement age raise the need for longevity insurance. The longer the retirement period, the greater the risk that retirees will outlive their resources and fall into poverty.

The Social Security benefits paid at age 62 are primarily old-age benefits. This type of benefit provides little longevity insurance at that age. As life expectancy at age 62 has increased, the proportion of Social Security benefits that serve the function of longevity insurance has decreased. By comparison, benefits paid starting at age 82 have a high component of longevity insurance.

## This Proposal

The longevity insurance benefit that I am proposing here is a delayed annuity in the form of a minimum Social Security benefit, which would be paid starting at age 82. That age would increase in the future as longevity increases. Age 82 is chosen because it is approximately the average life expectancy at age 65 (CDC 2007). Longevity insurance is primarily a benefit for women, since women outnumber men by roughly two to one in this age group (Smith 2003).

The longevity insurance would be a price-indexed annuity, just like current Social Security benefits. Thus, the deferred aspect of the annuity would not disadvantage recipients because there would be no loss of buying power from the annuity.

Recognizing this enhanced insurance protection, Social Security Old-Age and Survivors Insurance (OASI) would be renamed Social Security Old-Age, Survivors, and Longevity Insurance (OASLI). The renaming would help inform people about the benefit: it would positively frame the benefit as a form of insurance, rather than the benefit being thought of as an antipoverty benefit.

In addition to serving as insurance against outliving one's resources in advanced old age, longevity insurance can simplify the problem retirees face of planning asset decumulation. Many retirees have difficulty managing the spend-down of their assets over a retirement period of uncertain length, in part because of the inherent difficulty in planning for a long and uncertain period. The prevalence of this problem will increase in the future as people live longer and as an increasing percentage of retirees have 401(k) plans, which generally do not provide annuities. With a longevity insurance benefit, that planning problem is simplified. Instead of planning for an uncertain period, retirees can plan for the fixed period from the date of their retirement to the date at which they start receiving the longevity insurance benefit.

As well as assisting in planning, longevity insurance may help people who at advanced ages have difficulty managing their finances. At advanced ages, people are increasingly likely to need assistance in managing their finances because of declining mental ability and declining health. With longevity insurance, retirees have nothing to manage concerning the receipt of the benefits because the benefits are handled automatically by Social Security, generally with automatic deposit to their checking account. They have no checks to cash or investments to manage.

Webb, Gong, and Sun (2007) estimate that with longevity insurance provided at an advanced age, a substantial share of the longevity insurance provided by an immediate annuity can be obtained. A deferred annuity starting at age 85 provides more than half the longevity insurance of an annuity starting at age 65 (between 56 and 62 percent, depending on the degree of risk aversion in their examples), and at a fraction of the cost—roughly 15 percent. The authors calculate that a household planning to smooth consumption through its retirement would need to allocate only 15 percent of its age-60 wealth to a deferred annuity with payments starting at age 85. The remainder of its wealth it would hold in nonannuitized form to finance consumption from age 60 to 85. Much of the utility value to workers of annuitization comes from insuring against the possibility of running resources down to a very low level if one lives to be older than expected (Brown 2001).

## Part of a Larger Reform

Longevity insurance can be an important component of a reform to restore Social Security solvency. Reform likely will reduce the generosity of Social Security old-age benefits. Most reform packages that cut benefits across the board would raise elderly poverty (see, for example, Sarney [2008]). Thus, there would be a need to increase the generosity of some benefits to provide better targeting to vulnerable populations.

That goal could be achieved by providing longevity insurance benefits. For low-income persons, the effects of benefit cuts later in life when they are least able to work would be moderated.

This policy shifts Social Security resources toward persons who both are old and have low incomes. When this policy is enacted within a fixed budget constraint, without enhanced financing for Social Security, it would involve a transfer of resources from people who are young and relatively well-off to people who are old and relatively poor.

**Benefit Payment Structures**

Longevity insurance benefits can be structured in different ways, at different costs, and with different goals being served. Benefits can be universal or they can be targeted. Universal benefits provide longevity insurance without regard for need. Targeted benefits take into account need. Because they are targeted, they can be provided at lower total cost. Within those two categories for benefit eligibility, benefits can be based on Social Security benefit levels, years of contributions to Social Security, or age, or they can be flat benefits, being the same amount for everyone who qualifies. For example, if the benefit is universal, everyone aged 82 and older could receive the same flat amount. Alternatively, everyone aged 82 could receive the same amount, but the amount would increase slightly more than the rate of inflation for subsequent years, so that it increases in real value at older ages. If the benefit is targeted, it could be based on the recipient having worked a minimum number of years, with the amount increasing based on the number of years worked. While these options would provide longevity insurance in different ways, the next section proposes a targeted option.

**A Specific, Targeted Option**

The level of benefits provided by longevity insurance proposed here would be based on quarters of contributions to Social Security. A minimum of 20 years (80 quarters) of contributions would be required. At that level, a benefit of 70 percent of the poverty level for a single or married person, depending on the Social Security benefit received, would be provided. For each additional four quarters, the benefit would increase by 1.5 percent, so that someone who had worked 40 years (160 quarters) would receive a benefit equal to 100 percent of the poverty level. There would be no maximum number of quarters, so that someone who had worked 45 years would receive a benefit at 107.5 percent of the poverty level (Table 5.1).

This benefit formula, by taking into account quarters of coverage, supports the principle that Social Security rewards work. Persons with more years of work who qualified for a longevity insurance benefit would receive a higher benefit. It also establishes the principle that a poor person who has worked at least 40 years is guaranteed at least a poverty-level benefit in advanced old age. Thus, a poor person who has worked for many years and has contributed to Social Security is guaranteed a minimum level of income, and the dignity associated with that, in advanced old age. However, a factor that may possibly reduce the effectiveness of this benefit is that people with low lifetime earnings tend to have more years of zero earnings than people with higher lifetime earnings. People in the lowest quintile of family lifetime earnings have on average 9.1 years of zero earnings, compared to 2.4 years in the second-lowest quintile (Sarney 2008).

Social Security currently treats divorced spouses as though they had the cost saving advantages of economies of scale inherent in living with another person. They receive the same benefit as do spouses. The longevity insurance benefit would help divorced spouses whose former spouses were still living.

The benefit eligibility conditions set out here exclude people who receive low benefits for reasons other than a full career with low earnings. First, recipients receiving a low benefit who have fewer than 80 quarters of covered earnings would be excluded. Second, recipients

**Table 5.1 Relationship between Number of Years of Covered Work and Benefit Level for the Longevity Insurance Benefit**

| Number of years (quarters) of covered work | Benefit as a percentage of the poverty level |
|---|---|
| 20 (80) | 70.0 |
| 30 (120) | 85.0 |
| 40 (160) | 100.0 |
| 45 (180) | 107.5 |

SOURCE: Author's calculations.

receiving benefits from pension plans in noncovered employment in federal, state, or local government would generally be excluded because they would have insufficient quarters of coverage. Thus, people would be excluded who were affected either by the Government Pension Offset, which reduces the spouse's benefit for spouses who have a government pension and were not covered by Social Security, or by the Windfall Elimination Provision, which reduces the Social Security benefit for persons who have a government pension and were in a job that was not covered by Social Security (and thus they did not pay Social Security taxes).

Social Security has provided a minimum benefit in the past, but not a longevity insurance benefit. The minimum benefit was available to workers taking Social Security benefits at the early retirement age or any later age. Because it was not well-targeted to low-income workers with long careers of covered employment, it was eliminated for beneficiaries who became entitled in 1982 or later. A more targeted minimum benefit was created in 1972 and still exists, but is being phased out. Diamond and Orszag (2004) have proposed a new minimum benefit, available at the early retirement age, that has some features similar to the longevity insurance benefit proposed here. Their minimum benefit would require at least 20 years of covered work and would increase in value for each additional year of covered work, reaching 100 percent of the poverty threshold for workers with 35 years of covered work.

The longevity insurance benefit would improve the progressivity of Social Security by shifting resources toward a subset of low-income persons. It also provides insurance against negative shocks, which cause some people to have low Social Security benefits.

Longevity insurance provided automatically to a broad group of people years in the future avoids the problem of adverse selection in insurance markets. When longevity insurance is purchased privately, presumably only people with long life expectancy would purchase it, which would drive up its price because of adverse selection.

While a pure longevity insurance benefit would provide benefits to everyone reaching the target age, the targeted longevity insurance benefit proposed here also insures against low benefits in old age because it is a benefits-tested benefit. However, it does not consider all the resources available to older persons, but only their Social Security benefits. The advantage of this approach is that payment would be automatic, without requiring the recipient to apply for it. Thus, there would not be the problem of having a low take-up rate among the targeted population.

Low take-up is a problem with some benefits for older persons. An estimated 40 percent of the elderly who are eligible for Supplemental Security Income (SSI) benefits do not apply for them (Hoskins 2008). Declining cognitive ability may contribute to a low take-up rate at advanced older ages. For this reason SSI is not a good substitute for longevity insurance benefits. Longevity insurance would help make up for the shortcomings of SSI, and could replace it for the target group. Furthermore, it would not be stigmatized, given that the benefit would be described as a form of insurance, rather than as an antipoverty benefit. It would not be as targeted a benefit as it would if all resources were considered as a qualifying condition, but that type of administrative process is both expensive and intrusive.

### Cost Estimate

This section presents a rough cost estimate for the proposed benefit. In 2004, there were 7.3 million persons aged 80 and older receiving Social Security benefits (Social Security Administration 2006). The poverty threshold for a single person aged 65 or older in 2004 was $9,060 (U.S. Census Bureau 2010). Roughly 24 percent of Social Security beneficiaries aged 80 or older had annual benefits of less than the poverty threshold, while roughly 11 percent had annual benefits at less than 70 percent of the poverty threshold (based on interpolation, Table 5.2). Thus, roughly 1.75 million were below the poverty line.

Somewhat dated data (for 1993) indicate that of the retired Social Security beneficiaries living in poverty, 42 percent had worked between 21 and 40 years and 10 percent had worked for 41 or more years (Diamond and Orszag 2004; Olsen and Hoffmeyer 2002). More recent data for benefit recipients in 2004 indicate that fewer than 20 percent of recipients have less than 20 years of covered earnings (Pfau 2008). Thus, if 80 percent of the target population aged 82 and older had at least 20 years of service, that population in 2004 would be less than 1.4 million. For the cost calculations, we assume there would be approximately 1.4 million eligible persons.

Table 5.2  Social Security Benefit Recipients with Low Annual Benefits,
2004

| Annual Social Security benefit level ($) | Percentage of recipients | Cumulative percentage of recipients | Cumulative percentage of recipients below the poverty line |
|---|---|---|---|
| 1–999 | 0.6 | 0.6 | 2.5 |
| 1,000–1,999 | 0.6 | 1.2 | 5.0 |
| 2,000–2,999 | 0.8 | 2.0 | 8.3 |
| 3,000–3,999 | 1.2 | 3.2 | 13.3 |
| 4,000–4,999 | 2.3 | 5.5 | 22.9 |
| 5,000–5,999 | 3.5 | 9.0 | 37.5 |
| 6,000–6,999 | 4.5 | 13.5 | 56.3 |
| 7,000–7,999 | 5.6 | 19.1 | 80.0 |
| 8,000–8,999 | 4.8 | 23.9 | 100.0 |
| 9,000–9,999 | 7.4 | 31.3 | |

NOTE: Blank = not applicable.
SOURCE: Social Security Administration (2006).

The level of the longevity insurance benefit received depends on the level of the person's Social Security OASI benefit and the number of years the person or the person's spouse (in the case of survivor benefits) had worked. The data in Table 5.2 suggest that the average benefits would be less than $3,000 a year. If these people each received a supplemental benefit that averaged $3,000 a year, the cost would be approximately $4.2 billion a year. This figure is rough, but it indicates approximate cost. For perspective, consider that the annual cost of this benefit would be less than half of the monthly cost of the Iraq war in 2009.

The choice of a level of benefits involves tradeoffs between budgetary considerations if there are more generous benefits and social welfare considerations if there are less generous benefits. Setting a benefit at less than the poverty line for workers with less than a full career of work represents the thinking that Social Security is not intended to be the sole source of income for older persons, even though statistics indicate that it is for many older persons. Basing the level of benefits on the current poverty line recognizes the reality that that amount is the poverty measure used in the United States, flawed though it may be. If in future years the United States adopts a new poverty standard, at that time policymakers might want to consider using that standard for setting the level of the longevity insurance benefit.

## Who Else Would Be Affected?

The children of people in their eighties would be affected because they would have less financial responsibility for low-income parents. Provision of longevity insurance may affect family relationships. It may empower the poor elderly and raise their social standing within the household and within their families.

Because this benefit provides a form of insurance, it affects potential beneficiaries as well as actual beneficiaries. Thus, it provides insurance to a person with low Social Security benefits even if that person or the person's spouse does not survive to receive the benefit. While the probability that a single person would survive to receive the benefit is roughly 50 percent, the probability is higher that at least one person in a couple would survive to receive it.

In a broader philosophical sense, the insurance would benefit all Americans. While a person aged 50 with a career of high earnings would probably never directly benefit from the insurance, that person could have been born into a family with less advantaged circumstances, or they could have suffered from serious health problems, and their situation at age 50 could have been much different.

A possible unintended consequence is that guaranteed minimum benefits reduce the incentive to save for people who anticipate that they may qualify for those benefits. Since the qualifying condition is the level of Social Security benefits at age 82, the unintended consequence of people taking steps to qualify would be expected to be minimal. For example, a person could retire at age 62 rather than age 65, possibly qualifying himself for the higher benefit at age 82, but at the cost of lower benefits for 20 years. It is thus unlikely that longevity insurance would reduce labor supply at older ages.

Raising the level of Social Security benefits could have the consequence that some people no longer would be eligible for food stamps, Medicaid, housing allowances, and other programs for low-income older persons.

A possible unintended consequence is that picking the age of 82 would be unfair to African Americans because of their shorter life expectancy. However, at older ages the difference in life expectancy is less than at younger ages, and at age 65 the difference for white and African American women is less than two years. Furthermore, at age 65, the difference in life expectancy between males and females is greater than the difference between African Americans and whites (CDC 2007).

Another possible unintended consequence is that government-provided longevity insurance would displace privately provided longevity insurance offered by insurance companies. This outcome appears unlikely given that few companies offer the annuity and that not many people purchase annuities—in particular not many of the target population.

Provision of longevity insurance by the government for Social Security beneficiaries with low benefits could stimulate demand among higher-income retirees for private longevity insurance. The example set by the government could serve as an endorsement that would encourage higher-income persons to consider obtaining such insurance through their 401(k) plans or purchased privately.

Political support tends to be greater for social insurance than for public assistance, perhaps because of the broader base of people it helps. For that reason, political support for adequate benefits through longevity insurance may be greater than for Supplemental Security Income or for a minimum benefit framed as an antipoverty benefit.

## LONGEVITY INSURANCE IN THE PRIVATE SECTOR AND INTERNATIONALLY

Most U.S. life insurance companies do not provide longevity insurance annuities. These annuities are only available from a small number of insurance companies (Iwry and Turner 2008). Longevity insurance has been available since about 2005. It is offered by MetLife, Hartford, and New York Life Insurance Company. If a 65-year-old man invested $100,000 with MetLife's Longevity Income Guarantee annuity (the maximum benefit without death benefit), he would receive $83,000 a year starting at age 85. Inflation protection and a return-of-premium guarantee can increase the premium by as much as 50 percent (Greene 2008).

U.S. pension plan tax qualification rules make it difficult for 401(k) participants to purchase longevity insurance. The problem arises with the requirement that minimum distributions from a 401(k) plan start by April 1 of the year following the year the person turns age 70½. This requirement prevents a person from using the entire account balance, or a substantial part of it, to purchase an annuity starting at age 80 or 85. Changes in these minimum required distribution rules should be considered to encourage the purchase of longevity insurance.

A further problem with private sector provision of these benefits is the long delay between the purchase and the first receipt, which raises the risk that the insurance company might go bankrupt. While insurance companies are backed by state guarantee funds, these funds are inadequate to deal with the bankruptcy of a major insurance company, such as AIG.

Old-age benefits starting at advanced old ages are provided in a few countries. The United Kingdom provides a small old age allowance to persons aged 80 and older. Ireland pays a benefit of about $800 a year at age 80, called the Age 80 Allowance. That benefit is automatically received by persons receiving Irish social security pensions once they turn 80. Italy has a special supplement for low-income persons aged 75 and older (European Commission 2001). The Riester pensions in Germany are voluntary defined contribution plans that were enabled by a reform that took effect in 2002. They require that at retirement the participant purchase a longevity insurance annuity that begins payment at age 85 (Börsch-Supan and Wilke 2005). Singapore is considering adding such a requirement to its mandatory defined contribution system.

## CONCLUSIONS

With increased longevity, older retirees face an increased risk of ending life with insufficient resources to maintain their standard of living. In the United States, people with low Social Security benefits who are in their eighties are a particularly vulnerable group. At that age, few are able to compensate for their low benefits by working. As a matter of national policy, it is desirable that people in this age group, often called the old-old, be able to live with sufficient resources that they are able to enjoy the last years of their lives with dignity.

The target population for the proposal discussed here is people aged 82 or older with low Social Security benefits and long work histories. Age 82 is chosen because it is approximately the average life expectancy at age 65. Elderly poverty is particularly high among this age group—a third higher than for people aged 65–69. People in this age group are particularly at risk of falling into poverty even if they have not been in poverty earlier in life. They also have greater difficulty leaving poverty than people at younger ages.

Longevity insurance can be an important component of a policy package to restore Social Security solvency. Public policy changes likely will reduce the generosity of Social Security old-age benefits to restore solvency. If general benefit reductions, such as through longevity indexing of benefits as of retirement age, are combined with a new longevity insurance benefit, it may be possible to retain much of the longevity insurance that Social Security provides for low-income persons. For these persons, the effects of benefit cuts later in life, when such persons are least able to work, would be moderated. This policy shifts Social Security resources toward persons who both are old and have low incomes. It involves a transfer of resources from people who are relatively young and well-off to people who are old and have low incomes.

## POLICY RECOMMENDATIONS

This chapter recommends that a new type of Social Security benefit be provided, called longevity insurance. Longevity insurance would be a type of social insurance providing benefits to qualifying persons at an advanced age—initially set at age 82, but periodically increased to take into account future increases in life expectancy As retirees age, they face an increased risk of poverty as they spend down their non–Social Security assets. A longevity insurance benefit would be paid by Social Security starting at age 82 for people with at least 20 years of covered earnings and receiving Social Security benefits below a fixed level.

Payment would not require an application or a means test; it would occur automatically. This would be a targeted, cost-effective way of addressing poverty at advanced old age. It could be included in a reform package to restore Social Security solvency that contained benefit cuts, so that it would prevent benefit cuts from increasing poverty rates at advanced older ages.

# Part 3

# Pension Policy

# 6
# Defined Contribution Plans

## Encouraging Annuitization

Retirees risk outliving their assets. While Social Security provides a guaranteed lifetime benefit, it does not provide enough income for most retirees to maintain their preretirement standard of living. Accordingly, individuals who reach retirement with a 401(k) plan and without a traditional defined benefit plan generally need to convert at least part of their account balance to a flow of income to pay for their retirement consumption. Relatively few, however, actually do that. Only 10 percent of individuals with defined contribution plans annuitized their account balances when terminating employment at ages 60 to 64 and ages 65 to 69 (Gale and Dworsky 2006).

Defined contribution plans can pay old-age benefits in any, or a combination, of five basic ways: 1) a lump sum, 2) a life annuity, 3) a phased withdrawal (based on annual recalculation of life expectancy), 4) installment (term-certain) payments, or 5) ad hoc withdrawals. An annuity is a financial instrument that converts an account balance into a stream of periodic payments. With life annuities, workers receive periodic payments that continue until death. Life annuities, referred to here simply as annuities, insure workers against running out of money if they live longer than expected.

The U.S. pension system has shifted dramatically over the past 20 years from defined benefit plans to defined contribution plans, primarily 401(k) plans. While defined benefit plans traditionally provided benefits as annuities, most 401(k) plans do not provide that option. Historical data indicates that traditionally defined contribution plans have generally not provided annuities. For example, in 1985, only 29 percent of full-time participants in retirement savings and thrift plans had annuities as a payout option (Mitchell 1992). Defined contribution plans accrue benefits in the form of an account balance and typically pay benefits as a lump sum. Money purchase plans are required to provide the option of a joint and survivors annuity, but few participants choose that option (Advisory Council on Employee Welfare and Pension Benefit Plans 2005b). While 401(k) plans are permitted to make a joint and survivor benefit the normal form of benefit payment, relatively few do. In 2000, 33 percent of defined contribution plans offered annuities (Blostin 2003).

This chapter considers changes in policy and changes in features of annuities to expand the extent to which 401(k) plans offer annuities and participants choose them. It makes a distinction between two types of 401(k) plans. For 401(k) plans that are sole or primary plans, it recommends further requirements so that they will function as pension plans rather than as savings plans. For 401(k) plans that are secondary plans, it does not recommend any changes.

To summarize the chapter in broad generalities, four approaches can be used to increase the annuitization of 401(k) plans: 1) changes in public policy (laws and regulations), 2) changes in annuity products, 3) changes in marketing of annuities, and 4) changes in the advice people receive when planning for retirement.

## POLICIES ENCOURAGING WORKERS TO ANNUITIZE

Because of the insurance against outliving one's assets that annuities provide, many public policy analysts support public policy to encourage annuitization. This section considers policy options for encouraging workers to annuitize their 401(k) account balances.

### Mandatory versus Voluntary Annuitization

Mandatory annuitization is the only policy that assures that everyone obtains an annuity from their 401(k) account balance. Because trivial benefit payments would result, mandatory annuitization generally excludes small account balances. Mandatory annuitization need not require that full annuitization of the account balance occur at retirement. Some degree of mandatory annuitization, such as partial annuitization or annuitization at an older age, would help assure that workers would not outlive their retirement savings. Mandatory annuity purchases would reduce annuity prices by expanding the market to cover individuals regardless of health and life expectancy. Also, mandatory annuities would be less expensive to administer than voluntary annuities, as they would offer greater economies of scale and reduced enrollment costs.

The requirement of mandatory annuitization could be limited to defined contribution plans that are the primary plan provided to workers. Thus, if an employer also provided a defined benefit plan, annuitization would not be mandated for the secondary defined contribution plan.

A mandate, however, may not be in the best interest of all participants. Workers who have a high replacement rate from Social Security and workers with short life expectancy may be better off without a mandate. Since low-income and low-education workers tend to have shorter life expectancy and higher Social Security replacement rates than other workers because of the progressivity of the Social Security benefit formula, they as a group may be disadvantaged by an annuity mandate. Furthermore, mandatory annuitization could be problematic when annuities are calculated on a unisex basis, because men possibly could purchase larger annuities in the individual market. Another argument against mandates is an ideological one: some people oppose mandates as an unwanted government intrusion into the lives of Americans.

Mandates can take various forms. For instance, a weaker mandate would require that employers offer annuities as an option. Alternatively, a partial mandate could require that the portion of the account balance attributable to employer contributions be annuitized. A mandate could take effect after a period of phased withdrawal. Partial annuitization could be required so that at least a minimum level of benefits was provided. For example, annuitization could be required of the employer contribution and the investment earnings attributable to that contribution. The requirement could be extended to the portion of the accumulated balance due to government tax relief. Partial annuitization has the advantage that it provides a guaranteed floor of retirement income while allowing the worker to maintain liquidity and control over some assets.

An argument against mandating an annuity, or even mandating the provision by 401(k) plans of one, is that workers can easily obtain an annuity by purchasing one with their account balance. This option, however, has at least three drawbacks. First, a drawback for women is that the annuity would be available on gender-based pricing, which would increase its cost for women. Second, the annuity would be priced on an individual rather than a group basis, which would increase its cost for both men and women. Third, this option is less convenient than obtaining an annuity through the pension plan, which reduces the likelihood that workers would take it. Full mandatory annuitization could reduce participation in a voluntary defined contribution system, as long-lived people are relatively more likely to participate than those with shorter life expectations, given the requirement of mandatory annuitization (Davis 2004).

Perhaps in part because of the interest rate risk associated with converting an account balance to an annuity, many countries with mandatory individual accounts do not require that workers annuitize their account balances. Seven countries in Latin America with mandatory individual accounts allow their workers to choose between an annuity or phased withdrawals throughout retirement, while two countries mandate annuity purchases (Kritzer 2000). Countries that do not mandate annuitization generally mandate that benefits be withdrawn in an orderly fashion through phased withdrawals.

Switzerland mandates provision of pensions that are similar to cash balance plans. Each worker has an individual account to which interest is credited. Pension law sets the minimum contribution rate, the minimum interest crediting rate, and the manner in which account balances are converted to annuities at retirement. Benefits must be paid as an annuity except for small account balances.

A compromise would be to impose a limited mandate that preserves the options of employees and employers. Such a mandate, favored here, would require that all employers that offer a 401(k) plan as the sole plan (i.e., without also offering a defined benefit plan meeting minimum standards of generosity) offer an annuity as an option for workers.

## Default Options

Behavioral finance has shown that defaults can have an important effect on pension outcomes for workers. Some workers, when they are eligible to participate in a 401(k) plan, do not decide whether to participate. They end up not participating out of inaction, since nonparticipation is the default in their plan. This group is affected by inertia and procrastination, which is also called "status quo bias." Making participation the default appears to markedly increase the percentage of workers participating in 401(k) plans (Madrian and Shea 2001).

Inertia or procrastination by workers may be the result of a number of different mental processes (Turner and Verma 2007). For instance, workers in this group may take a passive approach to decision making (Choi et al. 2001). Or, they may have ambivalent feelings about the decision and for that reason not decide whether to enroll. Ambivalence and procrastination may also arise because of the complexity of the decision-making process—in particular, the complexity of the decision as to how to invest the pension funds, but also complexity in issues relating to how to take withdrawals.

The positive experience concerning worker participation rates with autoenrollment may appear to provide lessons for encouraging annuitization. Thus, it might be thought that making an annuity the default option could have an important effect on the percentage of pension participants taking annuities. For example, annuitization could be the default, with other forms of benefit receipt being allowed only if the participant's spouse agrees in writing. That approach is mandated for benefits provided by employer-sponsored defined benefit pension plans and money-purchase defined contribution pension plans, but not for 401(k) plans.

However, while defaults have a powerful effect on raising the participation rate among groups with low participation in 401(k) plans, defaults do not always have such a strong effect in other contexts. Because of the financial importance of the decision and its irreversibility, if annuities were the default, considerably more people might opt out of the default than has been the case with automatic enrollment. Anecdotal evidence strongly suggests that many workers opt out of the default of an annuity and take a lump sum distribution when that option is offered in traditional defined benefit plans.

It also appears that workers are much more likely to take lump sum distributions from cash balance plans than from traditional defined benefit plans. This observation may provide further evidence of the importance of framing, suggesting that workers are less likely to choose an annuity when the benefit is presented to them as an account balance than when it is presented to them as an annuitized benefit.

Defaults appear to have a larger impact on outcomes when the decision is of less consequence to the worker. If the amount of money committed at any point in time is small, and the implicit commitment to the default status for future purchases is reversible, defaults are more likely to affect workers.

This lesson from the experience with defaults concerning small purchases suggests a possible policy to encourage annuitization. A possible default for annuitization would be that workers would begin purchasing annuity units with their contributions starting at a particular age, say at age 40. Each pay period, part of their contributions would go toward purchasing annuity units. This default is likely to be more effective than a default at retirement because workers can opt out of later annuity purchases, and the amount they are purchasing at any one time is small. Workers would benefit from dollar cost averaging by purchasing annuities over time at different interest rates. This approach mitigates the conversion risk that occurs when the entire annuity is purchased at one point in time at retirement (Iwry and Turner 2009).

## Spousal Consent

Spousal consent is required in other pension decisions, so the principle is established that spousal consent can be used as a way of encouraging certain behavior, particularly when that behavior affects the spouse. For example, spousal consent is required in defined benefit plans if the participant takes an option other than a joint and survivor benefit. The choice of annuities in 401(k) plans could be encouraged by requiring spousal consent for an option other than an annuity with a joint and survivor benefit. Currently, if an annuity option is not provided, spousal consent is not required for withdrawing part or all of a worker's account balance. Alternatively, the plan could be required to notify the spouse if a different option were chosen. The pensions for federal government employees provide examples of these approaches. Federal government workers in the Thrift Savings Plan who participate in the Federal Employees Retirement System (the "new" system) have the first of these two alternatives for requirement of spousal consent. Federal government workers in the Thrift Savings Plan who participate in the Civil Service Retirement System (the "old" system) have the second requirement of spousal notification. The role of spousal consent may, however, be limited in its ability to influence couples to opt for annuities, as evidenced by the experience with cash balance plans, where consent is required but lump sums are commonly taken.

## Incentives

Incentives could encourage employers to offer annuities as an option in 401(k) plans. These incentives could include regulatory relief. Regulatory relief might take the form, for example, of allowing electronic spousal consent, which would enable plans to save costs by avoiding paper systems for spousal protections. Some participant-rights activists argue, however, that electronic spousal consent can easily be abused, because the quality of the signatures in currently available systems is too poor to allow verification as to who has signed.

Tax incentives are another means to encourage the use of annuities. Incentives can take the form of either more favorable tax treatment for annuities or less favorable tax treatment for lump sums and other forms of withdrawals. Tax advantages could be provided for plans that only provide annuities. They could be offered to workers that choose annuities. In Japan, pension annuities receive preferential income tax treatment: they are tax-free up to a certain amount per year, with a variable deduction that declines in percentage terms in increments for benefits exceeding a certain level.

Adding tax incentives for annuities, however, would raise the tax expenditures for the pension system. That would contribute further to federal budget deficits. These tax incentives would probably most benefit middle- and upper-income workers because those workers are most likely to have pensions. A bill proposed a few years ago, called the Lifetime Pension Annuity for You Act of 2005, would have provided defined contribution plan participants with a tax exemption on 25 percent of income from annuities purchased through qualified plans, up to $5,000. This ceiling would have limited to some extent the possible adverse distributional consequences of providing favorable tax treatment of annuities.

If tax incentives were provided for annuities, presumably they would apply to both defined benefit and defined contribution plans. However, if they did include both types of plans, that would increase further the lost tax revenue, with much if not most of the forgone revenue going to benefit participants in defined benefit plans, where workers generally already take annuities.

## Penalties

The opposite approach to providing tax incentives to take annuities is to provide penalties for not taking them. In 2006, Spain reduced the generosity of the tax treatment of lump sum benefits in order to encourage workers to purchase annuities (Social Security Administration 2007). However, to the extent that lower-income workers, who have lower life expectancy, do not take annuities, this approach would penalize them.

## Immediate Annuity with Programmed Withdrawals

Chile has an annuity package that combines an immediate annuity with programmed withdrawals (Social Security Administration 2004). The advantage of this annuity package is that it pays benefits for life but the balance of the account used for programmed withdrawals is inheritable if the person dies early. This combination allows participants to have both the advantages of guaranteed lifetime income through an annuity and the possibility of leaving an inheritance to their offspring.

## Insurance for Annuities

Annuity providers are insurance companies that are regulated in the United States at the state level. Each state provides a guarantee fund for annuities in case the insurance company should become insolvent, but the amount guaranteed varies by state, ranging from $100,000 to $500,000. Of greater concern is that the state insurance funds have insufficient assets to guarantee the failure of a large insurance provider, such as AIG. The United Kingdom, rather than having a patchwork of insurers of insurance companies, has a single insurer at the national level, the Financial Services Compensation Scheme. Annuities are insured at 90 percent of their value, with no ceiling.

## THE USE OF INFORMATION TO AFFECT BEHAVIOR: EDUCATION, FRAMING, AND ADVICE

Education, framing, and advice are options for encouraging workers to choose annuitization. Education involves providing information to participants. Framing relates to the way information is provided; it highlights more important information. Advice goes beyond education and framing and explicitly makes recommendations. These options all relate to the way information is presented to workers.

### Participant Education

Workers may need to be educated as to the advantages of guaranteed lifetime income provided by annuities. The Advisory Council on Employee Welfare and Pension Benefit Plans (2005a), an advisory group appointed by the Secretary of Labor, commented that plan communications tend to focus on the accumulation phase rather than on the payout phase. The council's report recommended that the Department of Labor provide guidance as to what constitutes education, as opposed to advice, when employers provide information concerning benefit options. Such guidance would alleviate concerns employers have over their fiduciary liability in providing such information to their workers.

Education for workers may need to include information about mortality risk and life expectancy in old age. Information concerning life expectancy is the most common way that information about mortality risk is provided. However, roughly half the population at retirement will outlive its life expectancy, so information about life expectancy sets a low standard in terms of the number of years that a person should be prepared to finance. It may be more useful, as far as helping participants understand the risks they face, to provide information on the probability that they will live to age 90, and the probability that at least one member of a couple will survive to age 90.

Participant education is often provided by the institution managing the investments of the participants' accounts, which is usually a mutual fund. Those institutions have an incentive to not provide information about the advantages of annuitization. Because they typically do not provide annuities, their income will be greater if participants continue to maintain an account balance that the mutual fund manages. Thus, policymakers may need to consider changing the incentives facing mutual fund companies as pension fund providers and as providers of education to 401(k) participants. For example, mutual fund companies could be paid a fee when an account holder annuitizes an account. However, unless the government provided a subsidy, this fee would ultimately be paid by the account holder, thus reducing the retirement income the account holder received.

The Pensions Advisory Service (2008), a part of the British government, provides a Web-based tool to help people understand the different options available from annuities and how those options would affect their level of benefits. This tool is designed to facilitate the choice of an annuity for people who do not have access to a financial adviser.

## Framing

The framing of the form of benefit receipt may be important. The concept of framing is that the way something is described is important to how it is perceived. Participants are accustomed to thinking of 401(k) plans in terms of their account balance. More participants might annuitize if they thought of their 401(k) plans in terms of the amount of annuitized income the account could provide. Thus, it might be desirable for quarterly statements to provide information as to the amount of annuitized income the account would provide if it were annuitized at a different age, such as at 62, 65, or 67. Expressing the value of an annuity this way would also have the advantage of clarifying to workers the value of postponing retirement. The Social Security Administration presents Social Security benefits this way on the annual individual statements it provides.

Several issues arise in attempting to accurately and clearly present the future annuitized value of a pension. The value presumably would be expressed based on the amount accumulated in the worker's account to date. To make it easier to interpret, it should be expressed in current dollars, rather than in future dollars, which would provide a misleadingly large figure because of inflation illusion. Since there is always uncertainty surrounding interest rates in the future, the value would best be presented as a range, or with some indication of the likely range of variability. Italy and the United Kingdom currently have this type of benefit reporting, where defined contribution plan participants receive an annual statement indicating the annuitized value of benefits accrued to date.

## Advice

Increasingly, pension participants have access to computer software that provides advice concerning planning for retirement. It is rare that any of this software advises users as to the benefits of annuitizing part of their accumulated assets (Turner and Witte 2009; Turner 2010b). Even when confronted with a hypothetical case contrived to make annuitization a desirable option, most free retirement planning software available over the internet does not advise annuitization (Turner 2010b).

## POLICY RECOMMENDATIONS

This chapter considers a number of options for encouraging annuitization so that more participants in 401(k) plans would receive benefits as a life annuity. Based on these options, we have five recommendations to make.

1) The first recommendation is to require that 401(k) plans offer annuities when those plans are provided by an employer that does not also provide a defined benefit plan meeting minimum standards of generosity. This requirement would treat 401(k) plans in that situation as pension plans rather than as savings plans, as they are currently treated.

2) The second recommendation is that 401(k) plans that are primary or sole plans be required to offer as an option the phased purchase of annuities while working. This option would be a considerably less risky way of purchasing annuities, compared to the current method of making a single purchase at retirement.

3) The third recommendation is that spousal consent be required for workers not choosing a joint and survivor annuity as the distribution form of their 401(k) account for 401(k) plans that

are primary or sole plans. This option presumably would be of particular benefit to women.

4) The fourth recommendation would be to require that pension annuities be covered by federal annuity insurance rather than by the inadequate, underfunded patchwork of insurance provided by the states.

5) Fifth, U.S. pension plan tax qualification rules make it difficult for 401(k) participants to purchase longevity insurance. The problem arises with the requirement that, to avoid tax penalties, minimum distributions from a 401(k) plan start by April 1 of the year following the year the person turns age 70½. This requirement prevents a person from using the entire account balance, or a substantial part of it, to purchase an annuity starting at age 80 or 85. Changes in these minimum required distribution rules should be considered to encourage the private purchase of longevity insurance.

# 7

# Defined Benefit Plans

## Flexibility to Deal with Increasing Life Expectancy

Improving longevity among workers causes the increasing social security costs that so many nations are facing, but it also causes increasing costs for employers sponsoring defined benefit plans. This increasing longevity raises the costs of providing benefits in defined benefit pension plans because workers receive benefits for more years. Defined benefit plans are traditional pension plans where the worker's benefit at retirement is typically based on a benefit formula that incorporates years of work and some measure of the worker's salary. Over a year, the effect on defined benefit plan costs of changes in life expectancy is small. Over a period of decades, however, the slow but continuous effect on pension costs of the cumulatively large increases in longevity can be considerable. This chapter considers policies to deal with the effects of increased longevity on defined benefit plans.

## EFFECT OF LIFE-EXPECTANCY INCREASES ON DEFINED BENEFIT PLAN COSTS

Life expectancy increased considerably during the latter half of the twentieth century. A 40-year-old man was expected to live to 73 in the 1980 population life table, but was expected to live to 78 in 2002 (Oster 2003). This change increases the length of retirement from 11 years to 16 years, assuming retirement at age 62—an increase in retirement years of 45 percent. Thus, it is plausible that life expectancy increases have had a substantial effect on the cost of defined benefit plans over the past 20 years.

Assuming an average retirement age of 62 in both 1980 and 2002, a 4 percent interest rate, and no inflation indexing of benefits past retirement, the growth in life expectancy since 1980 has increased the

117

nominal cost of providing a defined benefit plan per male participant by more than 30 percent. This number is less than the 45 percent increase in retirement years because of the effect of interest discounting, which reduces the present value of distant future benefits. Thus, over this period, defined benefit costs have grown by an average of more than 1 percent per year per male participant because of the increase in life expectancy. This number is a rough approximation, but it gives an estimate of the magnitude of the effect for a typical defined benefit plan. The "feminization" of some pension plans due to the increased labor force participation of women would further increase costs, since that would raise the average life expectancy of the participants in the plan.

Related evidence as to the effect of life expectancy on plan costs is provided by the price changes made by life insurers. Life insurers in the United States have revised downward their prices by amounts ranging from 10 to 30 percent because new mortality tables are being used that replace tables established in 1980 (Oster 2003).

In the United Kingdom, the effect of increasing longevity on defined benefit plan costs is thought to be one of the reasons why employers are ending those plans in favor of defined contribution plans (Pensions Policy Institute 2007). According to a British survey, the primary reasons for large numbers of employers terminating defined benefit pension plans are increased costs due to lower real investment returns and greater longevity (White 2003).

## The Effects of Uncertainty on Improvements in Life Expectancy

The uncertainty of the cost imposed by unknown future changes in longevity may also affect employers' pension decisions. Future improvements in life expectancy are inherently uncertain, causing employers sponsoring defined benefit plans to bear longevity risk. The dramatic rise in obesity in recent years may cause life expectancy to increase less than currently projected, or a revolution in medical science may cause the improvements to be greater than projected. As an example of the differences of opinion among experts, the Social Security actuaries projected that between 2000 and 2080 there would be an increase of six years for life expectancy at birth, but the 2003 Technical Panel on Assumptions and Methods (2003), which examined the basis for that projection, recommended projecting an even greater increase in life expectancy, about 7.5 years.

Pension plan sponsors during the late 1940s and 1950s, when many defined benefit plans were established, may have poorly anticipated improvements in life expectancy at older ages. The increases in life expectancy at older ages during the preceding decades were relatively small. Life expectancy at age 65 rose from 11.7 years in 1900 to 21.2 years in 2000, an 81 percent increase. However, 75 percent of this change occurred after 1950. The improvements in life expectancy at older ages generally accelerated over the century, thanks especially to an unprecedented reduction in mortality from cardiovascular disease beginning in the late 1960s (Technical Panel on Assumptions and Methods 2003).

## EMPLOYER PENSION RESPONSES TO INCREASED WORKER LONGEVITY

Increasing life expectancy raises pension liabilities based on both future and past work. Employers have a number of options for dealing with this problem, though some good ones are prevented by U.S. pension law (Muir and Turner 2007). Some employers aggressively deal with the problem by maintaining updated mortality tables; others use conservative funding assumptions to offset the misrepresentation of costs that an outdated mortality table yields; other employers cut future benefit accruals; and still others encourage their employees to take a lump sum option, which frees them of liability for future longevity improvements during the worker's retirement period. But in what is more often the case, firms are switching to defined contribution plans or cash balance plans, where employer costs are unaffected by the apparent glacial inevitability of improved longevity.

In adjusting defined benefit plans to offset the benefit cost increase caused by increasing life expectancy, employers can cut benefits received at normal retirement, cut early retirement benefits, reduce cost-of-living adjustments for benefits being paid, or raise the early or normal retirement ages, all of which are indirect ways of cutting benefits. Employers can end plan features that provide incentives for early retirement. In most countries, and in government-sector plans in the United States, employees as a general rule directly share in the financing of defined benefit plans by making mandatory tax-deductible contributions. Raising these contributions is another way of dealing with increased costs due to increased longevity. Besides making adjustments in defined benefit plans to offset the increased benefit cost due to increased longevity, employers may make other adjustments. Employers may reduce the amount of wage compensation they pay, so that the workers themselves absorb the increased cost of providing pension benefits through reduced wages.

Employers can reduce future pension accruals for new employees by establishing a higher early-retirement age or requiring more years of service to qualify for early retirement, but making these changes is administratively complex. The approach of basing changes on the date of employment has the further disadvantage that different employees who may be holding similar jobs are treated differently. Nonetheless, such an approach would be legal under pension law, and may be viewed by employees as fair, since it becomes part of the labor agreement at time of hire.

Employers can also reduce future pension accruals for current employees. When they do so, they must distribute an Employee Retirement Income Security Act (ERISA) Section 204(h) notice to employees, advising them of the change and explaining its effect on them. When the reduction is for an early retirement benefit, the notice must provide an explanation of the benefit before and after the change. More information is required if the simple description does not give a reasonable picture of the full impact of the change (Segal Company 2003). Although these notice provisions do not prohibit plan amendments that reduce accruals, they do ensure that participants are informed about pending changes. These disclosure requirements may discourage plan sponsors from taking actions that they would prefer not to highlight to their employees or may enable employees to exert pressure against potential plan amendments.

Relatively few sponsors of ERISA defined benefit plans have raised their early retirement age, in spite of large increases in cost due to significant increases in life expectancy (Muir and Turner 2007). However, some private-sector employers have established separate plans with higher early-retirement ages for new employees. In the government sector, the early retirement age has been increased in the federal government's plan for civil servants, as well as in some state and local government plans, especially for teachers. The evidence from the government sector provides some indication that the anticutback rule in ERISA may be making it difficult for private employers to adjust their defined benefit plans for the increased costs stemming from increasing longevity.

ERISA appears to have limited increases in the normal retirement age (NRA) by legislative language that has been interpreted by some pension attorneys to indicate that the NRA cannot be raised higher than age 65. Even if ERISA would permit such a change, its substantive and notice provisions may act as an implicit barrier.

## INTERNATIONAL SURVEY

International evidence may provide further insights into reasons why ERISA plans in the United States have not raised the early retirement age. The following survey of policies in different nations points to international experience that may be useful for the United States in considering policy options with respect to the early retirement age and the normal retirement age in occupational pension plans. By providing information about reforms in other countries, it may indicate the range of feasible reforms.

**Australia**. The minimum retirement age is 55 for receiving a pension benefit for both men and women born before July 1, 1960. It will gradually increase so that for those born after June 30, 1964, the minimum retirement age will be 60.

**Belgium**. In 2003, Belgium passed a pension law stipulating that pension benefits cannot be paid before the age of 60. Previously benefits could be received at age 58 or earlier. For all existing plans, the old rules applied until January 1, 2010 (Watson Wyatt Worldwide 2003).

**New Zealand**. New Zealand has passed human rights legislation that bans compulsory retirement ages. Before that legislation, the country's police departments had set a mandatory retirement age of 55 (Global Action on Aging 2003).

**Switzerland**. To make the early retirement age for social security pensions the same as that for occupational pensions, in 2001 Switzerland increased the early retirement age for occupational pension plans from age 62 to 64. The increase from 62 to 63 took place in 2001, and the increase from 63 to 64 took place in 2005.

**United Kingdom**. The United Kingdom has raised the minimum age at which occupational pensions can be received from 50 to 55. Civil servants became subject to a new early retirement age of 65 for all new employees starting in 2006; prior to that the pensionable age was 60.

**European Union**. Legislation proposed in 1999 and taking effect in May 2004 increased the retirement age for European Union civil servants from 60 to 63. However, up to 10 percent of the civil servants will be able to retire earlier under certain conditions (Spiteri 2003).

## A LIFE EXPECTANCY–INDEXED DB PLAN

A factor that appears to have led to the decline in defined benefit plans in the United States and elsewhere has been the increase in life expectancy. Defined benefit plans do not have the flexibility to deal readily with this continued increase in cost.

A policy innovation would permit life-expectancy indexing of benefits at retirement: a life expectancy–indexed DB plan. This innovation follows the Notional Defined Contribution plan in Sweden. A traditional defined benefit plan can easily be converted into a life expectancy–indexed DB by adding a single feature to the calculation of initial benefits at retirement. Each year as another cohort reaches retirement age, the generosity of benefits would be reduced slightly to take into account the continued improvement in life expectancy. The adjustment would not reduce expected lifetime benefits, but rather would offset the increase in lifetime benefits caused by increased life expectancy. No further adjustments would occur for life expectancy improvements during retirement. Thus, some of the cohort life expectancy risk would remain with employers.

Life expectancy risk can be divided into the idiosyncratic risk that a particular individual will live longer than expected and the cohort risk that an entire cohort on average will live longer than expected. Annuity providers are able to deal with idiosyncratic risk by pooling it across large numbers of people, effectively diversifying it away. However, cohort risk cannot be pooled because it is correlated across workers. Longevity bonds would provide a hedge, but a market for them has not developed. The higher the percentage of a cohort that remains alive, the higher the payout from longevity bonds. Life-expectancy indexing of benefits is one way of dealing with this risk. The idiosyncratic risk is borne by the annuity provider, who can diversify it away. The cohort risk is borne by workers, who are the beneficiaries of the improved life expectancy.[1]

A life expectancy–indexed DB plan would arguably provide more efficient bearing of longevity risk than a traditional defined benefit plan. Life-expectancy indexing of benefits would shift to workers the cohort life-expectancy risk, which is the risk that an entire birth cohort will live longer than expected, on average. The plan sponsor bears the idiosyncratic life-expectancy risk, which is the risk that a particular individual will live longer than expected.

Different pension types vary in the life expectancy risk that workers and employers bear (Table 7.1). In a traditional defined benefit plan, the employer bears both the idiosyncratic and the cohort risk. In a 401(k) plan without an annuity, the employee bears both of those risks. In a life expectancy–indexed DB plan and in a 401(k) plan with an annuity, the risks are shared, as employers bear the idiosyncratic risk and employees bear the cohort risk.

Under current U.S. pension law (ERISA), this innovation would not be allowed because it would violate the anticutback rule. The

**Table 7.1  Bearing of Longevity Risk by Employers, Employees, and Insurance Companies**

| Plan type | Idiosyncratic risk | Cohort risk |
|---|---|---|
| LE DB | Employer | Employee |
| Traditional DB | Employer | Employer |
| BMW's DB plan (UK) | Insurance company | Insurance company |
| 401(k) without annuity | Employee | Employee |
| 401(k) with annuity | Insurance company | Employee |

NOTE: "LE" stands for "life expectancy–indexed."
SOURCE: Author's compilation.

anticutback rule is defined in terms of annual benefits. If that rule were redefined to take an economist's perspective and use lifetime benefits as the measure, life-expectancy indexing would not constitute a cutback in lifetime benefits.

With this proposal, the risk that on average workers will live longer is largely shifted from employers to workers. Workers are better able to bear this risk than employers because they are also the beneficiaries of the increased life expectancy. They can adjust to the benefit cuts by working longer, which is facilitated by their increased life expectancy. An issue arises for plan sponsors as to who would generate the life expectancy index to be used. Department of Labor regulations may need to resolve that issue, setting a required index or a minimum standard.

A similar approach for dealing with cohort life expectancy risk, which may have the questionable advantage of being less transparent to workers, would be to index the plan's normal retirement age to increases in life expectancy. Doing so could also result in a reduction in annual benefits while maintaining the lifetime expected value of benefits. This change is less transparent because it is presented to workers as an increase in the normal retirement age rather than a cut in benefits.

A variant of this proposal has been adopted by BMW in the United Kingdom (Plumridge 2010). Under this arrangement, BMW has shifted the cohort and idiosyncratic longevity risk to a life insurance company, rather than shifting that risk to workers. It retains financial market risk.

## LIFE-EXPECTANCY INDEXING OF FIXED AGES IN PENSION LAW

U.S. pension law contains a number of fixed minimum or maximum ages for receipt of benefits. For example, retirees generally must start receiving benefits shortly after they turn age 70½. Another example is that they cannot receive benefits from a 401(k) plan before age 55 without a tax penalty and without having terminated employment with that employer, or age 59½ while continuing in employment with the same employer. Pension law is generally interpreted as not permitting a normal retirement age in defined benefit plans higher than age 65. Given the increase in longevity, it may make sense to periodically review and raise these ages or automatically index them.

## LUMP SUM BENEFITS IN DEFINED BENEFIT PLANS

While defined benefit plans are not required to provide a lump sum option, many of them do, presumably because participants like the option. Once a plan sponsor offers a lump sum distribution as an option in a defined benefit plan, ERISA makes it difficult for that option to be ended. Thus, a possible change in pension law would be to clearly allow employers to terminate the lump sum distribution option in defined benefit plans in order to encourage annuitization.

## POLICY RECOMMENDATIONS

This chapter recommends that pension law be amended to permit a new type of defined benefit plan, called a life expectancy–indexed DB plan. This plan would allow more efficient bearing of life expectancy risk than is currently permitted in defined benefit plans. With a life expectancy–indexed DB plan, at retirement the generosity of the plan would be adjusted to take into account improvements in life expectancy, analogous to annuitizing a defined contribution plan account using current life expectancy. Thus, cohort life expectancy risk would be shifted to workers, who can bear it more easily than plan sponsors because the workers are the prime beneficiaries of the increase in life expectancy.

In addition, this chapter recommends life-expectancy indexing: legally set minimum or maximum ages in pension law to take into account improvements in life expectancy. For example, the requirement that pension payments begin shortly after a person turns age 70½ would be periodically updated to take into account improvements in life expectancy. Similarly, pension law should be clarified so that a normal retirement age greater than 65 in defined benefit plans would be allowed. This chapter recommends that ERISA be clarified to permit defined benefit plans to terminate lump sum benefits as an option, in order to encourage annuitization.

## Note

1.  A study has attempted to quantify the aggregate mortality risk, which is the risk that an entire cohort will live longer than predicted (Friedberg and Webb 2005). The study estimates that a markup of the annuity premium by 4.3 percent would reduce the probability of insolvency due to cohort mortality risk to 5 percent, and that a markup of 6.1 percent would reduce the probability of insolvency to 1 percent.

# Part 4

# Conclusion

# 8
# Policy Recommendations

While increasing longevity at older ages is well known, U.S. policymakers have not developed a unified national policy that deals with its effects. In this book, I recommend a number of policies for dealing with increased longevity, arguing that a unified longevity policy would be more effective than dealing separately with the issues facing older workers, pensions, and Social Security. Together, these policies would encourage work at older ages, move Social Security toward solvency, provide better targeting of Social Security benefits, increase annuitization of 401(k) accounts, and encourage employers to provide defined benefit plans.

## POLICY RECOMMENDATIONS

Chapter 2 presents evidence concerning improvements in the ability of older persons to work and in reductions in the physical demands of many jobs. Based on that evidence, it appears clear that if older workers were economically motivated to do so and the demand for older workers were sufficient, it would be feasible for many to extend their work lives. This change could be facilitated by encouraging older workers to maintain and improve their job skills through training programs or informal training on the job. To facilitate such a policy, it also would be desirable to address barriers to employment at older ages. Many older workers report age discrimination if they are in the situation of looking for a job—for example, if they have been laid off. While this book does not address this issue, it recommends that further research be done on the issue of age discrimination and policies to deal with it. A further topic worth exploring is the issue of educating workers as to the benefits of postponing retirement. Deciding at what age to retire is one of the most important financial decisions a worker makes, yet it appears that many workers retire too early, perhaps because of myopia as to the consequences of the decision.

Recognizing the political difficulty in enacting reforms that involve cutting benefits, raising taxes, or raising the early retirement age, Chapter 3 recommends an automatic adjustment mechanism be adopted to help restore and maintain Social Security's solvency. The chapter recommends that Social Security benefits be indexed for life expectancy, so that increases in life expectancy would not cause an increase in the lifetime value of pension benefits. This type of indexation has been adopted by Sweden for its social security program.

With this type of indexation, every year for each new retirement cohort, benefits would be slightly adjusted downward to take into account the effect of increased life expectancy on the lifetime value of benefits. The adjustment would occur for each cohort only once, with benefits received at retirement facing no further adjustments for continued increases in life expectancy during the retirement period. This type of indexation results in a reduced replacement rate over time. Chapters 4 and 5 address that issue.

Based on the evidence presented in Chapter 2 indicating that the early retirement age could be raised with relatively little hardship for most workers, Chapter 4 recommends that the early retirement age for Social Security be raised to 63, with that change being phased in starting in 15 years, and that thereafter the early retirement age be automatically adjusted to take into account continuing improvements in life expectancy. This change could offset to some extent the benefit cuts recommended above, so as to diminish the reduction in annual benefits workers would receive. The initial change would occur at the rate of two months every other year, so that for persons aged 47 the new early retirement age would be 62 years and two months; for persons aged 45 it would be 62 years and four months; and so on. This policy would be enacted with a long lead time and phase-in period so as to allow people time to plan for the change. It thus would not affect workers nearing retirement and would only affect workers in the future, when it can be expected that life expectancy will be even longer than it is now.

As a matter of social policy concern for vulnerable groups, it would be desirable to consider other changes to help a small group of vulnerable workers who are unable to extend their work lives. While this group of workers is often cited as a reason not to raise the early retirement age, the group is small, and policies can be enacted that address their particular needs. These policies could include early benefits for workers with many years of covered Social Security work or lowering the requirements for receipt of disability benefits at older ages.

If the early retirement age was raised to help restore solvency, the benefits received at the new early retirement age would be the same as those currently receivable at age 62. This change would encourage workers to postpone retirement, thus reducing Social Security's deficit. Alternatively, if this change were done in conjunction with the recommended life-expectancy indexing of benefits, the benefits receivable at age 63 would be unchanged, being the same as those receivable at 63 before the increase in the early retirement age.

While some people are adamantly opposed to any cuts in Social Security benefits because those benefits already are not generous by international standards, others are equally adamant that there should be no increases in taxes to support Social Security. Once both groups realize that some change is needed and it is a matter of making a choice of which one, perhaps raising the early retirement age with a long lead time might be less unpopular than the two alternatives. While some people object to such a policy as placing a hard burden on workers, those making that criticism seem to be unaware that when President Franklin Roosevelt signed the Social Security Act in 1935, and for more than 20 years afterward, during an era when life expectancy was lower and more people had physically demanding jobs, the early retirement age was 65.

If the early retirement age is raised, the same arguments justifying that change should also lead to an increase in the maximum age for actuarial increases in benefits with postponed receipt of benefits. Currently, benefits are adjusted for postponement of receipt up to age 70. If the early retirement age is increased to age 63, the maximum age for actuarial adjustment should be raised to 71.

Taking steps to address low income at older ages, Chapter 5 recommends that a new type of Social Security benefit be provided called longevity insurance. Longevity insurance would be a type of social insurance providing benefits to qualifying persons at an advanced age —initially set at age 82, but automatically increased to take into account future increases in life expectancy.

As retirees age, they face an increased risk of poverty as they spend down their non–Social Security assets. A longevity insurance benefit would be paid by Social Security starting at age 82 for people with at least 20 years of covered earnings and receiving Social Security benefits below a fixed level. Payment would not require an application or a means test; it would occur automatically. This would be a targeted, cost-effective way of addressing poverty at advanced old age.

Longevity insurance could be included in a reform package to restore Social Security solvency that contained benefit cuts, so that it would prevent benefit cuts from increasing poverty rates at advanced older ages. It would be financed out of payroll tax revenue. Thus either payroll taxes would need to be higher than otherwise in order to finance it, or other benefit cuts could provide the needed financing.

Chapters 6 and 7 consider longevity policy options for employer-provided pension plans. Chapter 6 considers a number of options for encouraging annuitization of 401(k) plan accounts so that participants would receive benefits as a life annuity. The first recommendation is to require that 401(k) plans offer annuities when those plans are provided by an employer that does not also provide a defined benefit plan meeting minimum standards of generosity. This requirement would treat 401(k) plans that are the primary plan as pension plans rather than as savings plans, as they are currently treated.

The second recommendation is that 401(k) plans that are sole or primary plans be required to offer as an option the phased purchase of annuities by the employee during that employee's working years. This option would be a considerably less risky way of purchasing annuities, compared to the current method of making a single purchase at retirement.

The third recommendation is that spousal consent be required for workers not choosing a joint and survivor annuity as the distribution form of their 401(k) account when the 401(k) plan is the sole or primary plan.

The fourth recommendation would require that pension annuities be covered by federal annuity insurance rather than by the inadequate, underfunded patchwork of insurance provided by the states.

Fifth, U.S. pension plan tax qualification rules make it difficult for 401(k) participants to purchase longevity insurance with their pension assets. The problem arises with the requirement that minimum distributions from a 401(k) plan start by April 1 of the year following the year the person turns age 70½. This requirement prevents a person from using the entire account balance, or a substantial part of it, to purchase an annuity starting at age 80 or 85. Changes in these minimum required distribution rules would facilitate the purchase of longevity insurance.

Because of the different types of risks that defined benefit and defined contribution plans impose on participants, a pension system would be better diversified if it provided both defined benefit and defined contribution plans to most workers. Defined benefit plans have declined, and currently most workers with a pension plan only have a defined contribution plan. In order to encourage employer provision of defined benefit plans, Chapter 7 recommends that pension law be amended to permit a new type of defined benefit plan, called a life expectancy–indexed DB plan. This plan would allow more efficient bearing of life expectancy risk than is currently permitted in defined benefit plans.

With a life expectancy–indexed DB plan, at retirement the generosity of the plan would be adjusted to take into account improvements in life expectancy, analogous to annuitizing a defined contribution plan account using current life expectancy or to the changes proposed for indexing Social Security benefits. Thus, cohort life expectancy risk would be shifted to workers, who can bear it more easily than plan sponsors because the workers are the prime beneficiaries of the increase in life expectancy.

In addition, this chapter recommends life expectancy indexing–fixed ages in pension law, so as to take into account improvements in life expectancy. U.S. pension law contains a number of fixed minimum or maximum ages for receipt of benefits. For example, the requirement that pension payments begin shortly after a person turns age 70½ would be periodically updated to take into account improvements in life expectancy. Similarly, pension law should be clarified so that a normal retirement age greater than 65 would be allowed for defined benefit plans. Furthermore, this chapter recommends that ERISA be clarified to permit defined benefit plans to terminate lump sum benefits as an option, in order to encourage annuitization.

## CONCLUSIONS

While the book argues for a number of distinct policies, its main argument is for a package of longevity policies. These policies would reinforce each other and would facilitate the adjustment of workers and pension systems to the costs and benefits of a longer life. A unified package of reforms dealing with longevity would not only be more effective, it would presumably be more feasible to enact from a political perspective, because it would provide a more balanced approach.

# References

Advisory Council on Employee Welfare and Pension Benefit Plans. 2005a. *Report of the Working Group on Retirement Distributions and Options.* Washington, DC: U.S. Department of Labor, Employee Benefits Security Administration. http://www.dol.gov/ebsa/publications/ac_1105a_report .html (accessed February 7, 2011).

———. 2005b. "Summary of Testimony by John Kimpel, Senior Vice President and Deputy General Counsel, Fidelity Investments." Contained in *Report of the Working Group on Retirement Distributions and Options.* Washington, DC: U.S. Department of Labor, Employee Benefits Security Administration. http://www.dol.gov/ebsa/publications/ac_1105a_report .html (accessed February 9, 2011).

Alho, Juha M., Jukka Lassila, and Tarmo Valkonen. 2006. "Demographic Uncertainty and Evaluation of Sustainability of Pension Systems." In *Pension Reform: Issues and Prospects for Non-Financial Defined Contribution (NDC) Schemes,* Robert Holzmann and Edward Palmer, eds. Washington, DC: World Bank, pp. 95–112.

Alpert, Andrew, and Jill Auyer. 2003. "The 1988–2000 Employment Projections: How Accurate Were They?" *Occupational Outlook Quarterly* 47(1): 2–21.

American Academy of Actuaries. 2006. "Longevity and Retirement Policy: Modernizing America's Retirement Programs to Keep Pace with Longevity." Issue brief. Washington, DC: American Academy of Actuaries. http://www .actuary.org/pdf/pension/retire_april06.pdf (accessed February 1, 2011).

Arias, Elizabeth, Lester R. Curtin, Rong Wei, and Robert N. Anderson. 2008. "U.S. Decennial Life Tables for 1999–2001, United States Life Tables." *National Vital Statistics Reports* 57(1): 1–40.

Australian Institute of Health and Welfare. 2005. "Obesity and Workplace Absenteeism among Older Australians." *Bulletin* 31(October): 1–15. http://www.aihw.gov.au/publications/aus/bulletin31/bulletin31.pdf (accessed February 1, 2011).

Blostin, Allan P. 2003. "Distribution of Retirement Income Benefits." *Monthly Labor Review* 126(4): 3–9.

Börsch-Supan, Axel H., and Christina B. Wilke. 2005. "Reforming the German Public Pension System." Paper presented at the American Economic Association Annual Meeting, held in Boston, January 6–8. http://www.rand.org/ content/dam/rand/www/external/labor/aging/rsi/rsi_papers/2006_axel1.pdf (accessed March 31, 2011).

Brooksbank, Daniel. 2003. "Netherlands Scraps Early Retirement Tax Breaks." *Investment and Pensions Europe*, September 17. http://www .ipe.com/news/netherlands-scraps-early-retirement-tax-breaks_7801 .php?s=netherlands%20scraps (accessed February 1, 2011).

Brown, Jeffrey R. 2001. "Redistribution and Insurance: Mandatory Annuitization with Mortality Heterogeneity." CRR Working Paper No. 2001-02. Chestnut Hill, MA: Center for Retirement Research at Boston College.

Brown, Robert L. 2008. "Reforms to Canadian Social Security, 1996–7." In *Lessons from Pension Reform in the Americas,* Stephen J. Kay and Tapen Sinha, eds. Oxford: Oxford University Press, pp. 242–256.

Burkhauser, Richard V., Kenneth A. Couch, and John W. Phillips. 1996. "Who Takes Early Social Security Benefits? The Economic and Health Characteristics of Early Beneficiaries." *Gerontologist* 36(6): 789–799.

Burkhauser, Richard V., and Ludmila Rovba. 2009. "Institutional and Individual Responses to Structural Lag: The Changing Patterns of Work at Older Ages." In *Aging and Work: Issues and Implications in a Changing Landscape*, Sara J. Czaja and Joseph Sharit, eds. Baltimore: Johns Hopkins University Press, pp. 9–34.

Burton, Wayne N., Chin-Yu Chen, Alyssa B. Schultz, and Dee W. Edington. 1998. "The Economic Costs Associated with Body Mass Index in a Workplace." *Journal of Occupational and Environmental Medicine* 40(9): 786–792.

Butrica, Barbara A., and Sheila R. Zedlewski. 2008. *More Older Americans Are Poor Than the Official Measure Suggests*. Older Americans' Economic Security Series, No. 15. Washington, DC: Urban Institute. http://www .urban.org/UploadedPDF/411670_older_americans.pdf (accessed February 3, 2011).

Capretta, James C. 2006. "Building Automatic Solvency into U.S. Social Security: Insights from Sweden and Germany." Brookings Policy Brief No. 151. Washington, DC: Brookings Institution.

Centers for Disease Control and Prevention (CDC). 2003a. *National Diabetes Fact Sheet*. Atlanta: Centers for Disease Control and Prevention. http://www.cdc.gov/diabetes/pubs/pdf/ndfs_2003.pdf (accessed February 3, 2011).

———. 2003b. "Public Health and Aging: Trends in Aging—United States and Worldwide." *Morbidity and Mortality Weekly Report* 52(6): 101–106. http://www.cdc.gov/mmwr/preview/mmwr-html/mm5206a2.htm (accessed February 3, 2011).

———. 2007. "QuickStats: Life Expectancy at Age 65 Years, by Sex and Race—United States, 1999–2004." *Morbidity and Mortality Weekly Report* 56(7): 147. http://www.cdc.gov/mmwR/preview/mmwrhtml/mm5607a5.htm (accessed February 3, 2011).

Chapman, Steven H., Mitchell P. LaPlante, and Gail Wilensky. 1986. "Life Expectancy and Health Status of the Aged." *Social Security Bulletin* 49(10): 24–48.

Chen, Yung-Ping, and John C. Scott. 2003. "Gradual Retirement: An Additional Option in Work and Retirement." *North American Actuarial Journal* 7(3): 62–74.

Choi, James J., David Laibson, Brigitte Madrian, and Andrew Metrick. 2001. "Defined Contribution Pensions: Plan Rules, Participant Decisions, and the Path of Least Resistance." NBER Working Paper No. 8655. Cambridge, MA: National Bureau of Economic Research.

Congressional Budget Office (CBO). 1999. *Raising the Earliest Eligibility Age for Social Security Benefits*. Washington, DC: Congressional Budget Office. http://www.cbo.gov/ftpdocs/10xx/doc1058/ssage.pdf (accessed February 7, 2011).

———. 2005. *Projected Effects of Various Provisions on Social Security's Financial and Distributional Outcomes*. Washington, DC: Congressional Budget Office. http://www.cbo.gov/ftpdocs/63xx/doc6377/Social_Security_Menu-CBO_baseline.pdf (accessed February 7, 2011).

Costa, Dora L. 2002. "Changing Chronic Disease Rates and Long-Term Declines in Functional Limitation among Older Men." *Demography* 39(1): 119–138.

Cutler, David M., Jeffrey B. Liebman, and Seamus Smyth. 2006. "How Fast Should the Social Security Eligibility Age Rise?" NBER Retirement Research Center Working Paper No. NB04-05. Cambridge, MA: Harvard University and National Bureau of Economic Research.

Davis, E. Philip. 2004. "Is There a Pension Crisis in the UK?" Pensions Institute Discussion Paper PI-0401. London: Pensions Institute. http://www.pensions-institute.org/workingpapers/wp0401.pdf (accessed February 7, 2011).

Diamond, Peter A., and Peter R. Orszag. 2004. *Saving Social Security: A Balanced Approach*. Washington, DC: Brookings Institution.

Employee Benefit Research Institute (EBRI), American Savings Education Council (ASEC), and Mathew Greenwald and Associates (Greenwald). 2003. *The 2003 Retirement Confidence Survey*. Washington, DC: Employee Benefit Research Institute, American Savings Education Council, and Mathew Greenwald and Associates. http://www.ebri.org/pdf/surveys/rcs/2003/03rcssof.pdf (accessed February 1, 2011).

European Commission. 2001. *Comparative Tables on Social Protection in the 25 Member States of the European Union, in the European Economic Area, and in Switzerland*. Brussels: European Commission. http://ec.europa.eu/employment_social/social_protection/missoc_tables_archives_en.htm#2001 (accessed February 7, 2011).

Fiebelkorn, Ian C. 2006. "The Economics of Obesity: Improved Health Pro-files among Obese Patients May Spur Higher Health Care Costs." *Health Promotion Economics* 1(2): 1–4.

Flegal, Katherine M., Margaret D. Carroll, Cynthia L. Ogden, and Lester R. Curtin. 2010. "Prevalence and Trends in Obesity among U.S. Adults, 1999–2008." *Journal of the American Medical Association* 303(3): 235–241. http://jama.ama-assn.org/cgi/content/full/2009.2014 (accessed February 8, 2011).

Freedman, Vicki A., Eileen M. Crimmins, Robert F. Schoeni, Brenda C. Spillman, Hakan Aykan, Ellen Kramarow, Kenneth C. Land, James Lubitz, Kenneth G. Manton, Linda G. Martin, Diane Shinberg, and Timothy Waidmann. 2004. "Resolving Inconsistencies in Trends in Old-Age Dis-ability: Report from a Technical Working Group." *Demography* 41(3): 417–441.

Freedman, Vicki A., Linda G. Martin, and Robert F. Schoeni. 2002. "Recent Trends in Disability and Functioning among Older Adults in the United States: A Systematic Review." *Journal of the American Medical Associa-tion* 288(24): 3137–3146.

Friedberg, Leora, and Anthony Webb. 2005. "Life is Cheap: Using Mortal-ity Bonds to Hedge Aggregate Mortality Risk." CRR Working Paper No. 2005-13. Boston: Center for Retirement Research at Boston College. http://escholarship.bc.edu/cgi/viewcontent.cgi?article=1107&context=retirement_papers (accessed February 1, 2011).

Gale, William G., and Michael Dworsky. 2006. "Effects of Public Policies on the Disposition of Lump-Sum Distributions: Rational and Behavioral Influences." CRR Working Paper No. 2006-15. Chestnut Hill, MA: Center for Retirement Research at Boston College. http://escholarship.bc.edu/cgi/viewcontent.cgi?article=11250context=retirement_papers (accessed Febru-ary 8, 2011).

Gebhardtsbauer, Ron. 1998. "Testimony of Ron Gebhardtsbauer, FSA, Senior Pension Fellow, American Academy of Actuaries." U.S. Congress. House of Representatives. Committee on Ways and Means. Hearing on *The Future of Social Security for This Generation and the Next: Increasing the Re-tirement Age*. 105th Cong., 2d sess., pp. 1–10. http://www.actuary.org/pdf/socialsecurity/ss_future.pdf (accessed February 8, 2011).

Global Action on Aging. 2003. *Retirement Age Chewed Over*. New York: Global Action on Aging. http://www.globalaging.org/pension/world/meatworker.htm (accessed March 24, 2011).

Goss, Stephen C. 2003. "Estimates of Financial Effects for a Proposal to Re-store Solvency to the Social Security Program—Information." October 8 memorandum to Peter Diamond, Professor, Massachusetts Institute of Technology, and Peter Orszag, Senior Fellow, Brookings Institution. From

Stephen C. Goss, Chief Actuary. Washington, DC: Social Security Administration.

———. 2010. "The Future Financial Status of the Social Security Program." *Social Security Bulletin* 70(3): 111–125.

Greene, Kelly. 2008. "How to Bulletproof Your Nest Egg." *Wall Street Journal*, June 14, R:1. http://online.wsj.com/article/SB121259350492445223.html (accessed February 7, 2011).

Hill, Catherine, and Virginia P. Reno. 2005. "The Financial Case for Late Retirement." In *In Search of Retirement Security: The Changing Mix of Social Insurance, Employee Benefits, and Individual Responsibility,* Teresa Ghilarducci, Van Doorn Ooms, John L. Palmer, and Catherine Hill, eds. New York: Century Foundation Press, pp. 9–24.

Hill, Tomeka M. 2010. "Why Doesn't Every Employer Have a Phased Retirement Program?" *Benefits Quarterly* 26(4): 29–39.

Hoskins, Dalmer D. 2008. "Tackling Old-Age Poverty in a Contributory Pension Program." PowerPoint presentation at the World Bank–Hitotsubashi–MOF workshop "Closing the Coverage Gap: The Role of Social Pensions," held in Tokyo, February 20–22.

Hutchens, Robert M., and Jennjou Chen. 2007. "The Role of Employers in Phased Retirement: Opportunities for Phased Retirement among White-Collar Workers." In *Work Options for Older Americans,* Teresa Ghilarducci and John Turner, eds. Notre Dame, IN: University of Notre Dame Press, pp. 95–118.

Iwry, J. Mark, and John A. Turner. 2008. "Expanding the Use of Annuities by 401(k) Participants: Innovations in Policy, Products, Marketing, and Advice." Draft paper. Washington, DC: Retirement Security Project.

———. 2009. "Automatic Annuitization: New Behavioral Strategies for Expanding Lifetime Income in 401(k)s." In *Automatic: Changing the Way America Saves*, William G. Gale, J. Mark Iwry, David C. John, and Lina Walker, eds. Washington, DC: Brookings Institution Press, pp. 151–170.

Johnson, Richard W. 2004. "Trends in Job Demands among Older Workers, 1992–2002." *Monthly Labor Review* 127(7): 48–56. http://www.bls.gov/opub/mlr/2004/07/art4full.pdf (accessed March 15, 2011).

Kirsch, Irwin, Henry Braun, Kentaro Yamamoto, and Andrew Sum. 2007. *America's Perfect Storm: Three Forces Changing Our Nation's Future.* Princeton, NJ: Educational Testing Service. http://www.ets.org/Media/Education_Topics/pdf/AmericasPerfectStorm.pdf (accessed February 9, 2011).

Könberg, Bo, Edward Palmer, and Annika Sundén. 2006. "The NDC Reform in Sweden: The 1994 Legislation to the Present." In *Pension Reform: Issues and Prospects for Non-Financial Defined Contribution (NDC) Schemes,*

Robert Holzmann and Edward Palmer, eds. Washington, DC: World Bank, pp. 449–466.

Korczyk, Sophie M. 2002. "Back to *Which* Future: The U.S. Aging Crisis Revisited." Issue Brief No. 2002-18. Washington, DC: AARP Public Policy Institute.

Kritzer, Barbara E. 2000. "Social Security Privatization in Latin America." *Social Security Bulletin* 63(2): 17–37.

Lakdawalla, Darius N., Jayanta Bhattacharya, and Dana P. Goldman. 2004. "Are the Young Becoming More Disabled?" *Health Affairs* 23(1): 168–176. http://content.healthaffairs.org/content/23/1/168.full (accessed February 10, 2011).

Lee, Sunhwa, and Lois Shaw. 2008. *From Work to Retirement: Tracking Changes in Women's Poverty Status.* AARP Public Policy Institute Research Report No. 2008-03. Washington, DC: AARP Public Policy Institute. http://assets.aarp.org/rgcenter/econ/2008_03_poverty.pdf (accessed February 10, 2011).

Leonesio, Michael V., Denton R. Vaughan, and Bernard Wixon. 2003. *Increasing the Early Retirement Age under Social Security: Health, Work, and Financial Resources.* Health and Income Security for an Aging Workforce Series, No. 7. Washington, DC: National Academy of Social Insurance. http://www.nasi.org/usr_doc/nasiBrief_risk7_03.pdf (accessed February 10, 2011).

Liebman, Jeffrey, Maya MacGuineas, and Andrew Samwick. 2005. *Nonpartisan Social Security Reform Plan.* Cambridge, MA: Harvard University, John F. Kennedy School of Government. http://www.hks.harvard.edu/jeffreyliebman/lms_nonpartisan_plan_description.pdf (accessed February 10, 2011).

Lindell, Christina. 2003. "Longevity Is Increasing—What about the Retirement Age?" Finnish Centre for Pensions Working Paper No. 6. Presented at the Fourth International Research Conference on Social Security, held in Antwerp, May 5–7.

Luxembourg Income Study. 2007. *LIS Key Figures.* Luxembourg: Luxembourg Income Study. http://www.lisproject.org/key-figures/key-figures.htm (accessed March 16, 2011).

Madrian, Brigitte C., and Dennis F. Shea. 2001. "The Power of Suggestion: Inertia in 401(k) Participation and Savings Behavior." *Quarterly Journal of Economics* 116(4): 1149–1187.

Maestas, Nicole, and Julie Zissimopoulos. 2010. "How Longer Work Lives Ease the Crunch of Population Aging." *Journal of Economic Perspectives* 24(1): 139–160.

Mermin, Gordon B.T., Richard W. Johnson, and Dan Murphy. 2006. "Why Do Boomers Plan to Work So Long?" Retirement Project Discussion Paper No. 06-04. Washington, DC: Urban Institute.

Mermin, Gordon B.T., and C. Eugene Steuerle. 2006. "Would Raising the Social Security Retirement Age Harm Low-Income Groups?" Issue Brief No. 19. Washington, DC: Urban Institute.

MetLife Mature Market Institute. 2008. *MetLife Retirement Income IQ Study: A Survey of Pre-Retiree Knowledge of Financial Retirement Issues.* New York: MetLife Mature Market Institute. http://www.metlife.com/assets/cao/ mmi/publications/studies/MMI-Studies-Retirement-IQ.pdf (accessed February 1, 2011).

Milevsky, Moshe A. 2005. "Real Longevity Insurance with Deductible: Introduction to Advanced-Life Delayed Annuities (ALDA)." *North American Actuarial Journal* 9(4): 109–122. http://www.soa.org/library/ journals/north-american-actuarial-journal/2005/october/naaj0504-8.pdf (accessed March 31, 2011).

Mitchell, Olivia S. 1992. "Trends in Pension Benefit Formulas and Retirement Provisions." In *Trends in Pensions 1992*, John A. Turner and Daniel J. Beller, eds. Washington, DC: U.S. Department of Labor, Pension and Welfare Benefits Administration, pp. 177–216.

Monk, Courtney, John A. Turner, and Natalia A. Zhivan. 2010. "Adjusting Social Security for Increasing Life Expectancy: Effects on Progressivity." CRR Working Paper No. 2010-9. Chestnut Hill, MA: Center for Retirement Research at Boston College.

Muir, Dana, and John A. Turner. 2007. "Longevity and Retirement Age in Defined Benefit Pension Plans." In *Work Options for Older Americans,* Teresa Ghilarducci and John A. Turner, eds. Notre Dame, IN: University of Notre Dame Press, pp. 212–231.

Munnell, Alicia H. 2003. *The Declining Role of Social Security.* Just the Facts on Retirement Issues Series, No. 6. Chestnut Hill, MA: Center for Retirement Research at Boston College.

Munnell, Alicia H., Kevin B. Meme, Natalia A. Zhivan, and Kevin E. Cahill. 2004. "Should We Raise Social Security's Earliest Eligibility Age?" Issue in Brief No. 18. Chestnut Hill, MA: Center for Retirement Research at Boston College.

Murray, Christopher J.L., Sandeep C. Kulkarni, Catherine Michaud, Niels Tomijima, Maria T. Bulzacchelli, Terrell J. Iandiorio, and Majid Ezzati. 2006. "Eight Americas: Investigating Mortality Disparities across Races, Counties, and Race-Counties in the United States." *PLoS Medicine* 3(9): 1513–1524. http://www.plosmedicine.org/article/info:doi/10.1371/journal .pmed.0030260 (accessed March 23, 2011).

National Academy on an Aging Society. 2000. *Diabetes: A Drain on U.S. Resources.* Challenges for the 21st Century: Chronic and Disabling Conditions Series, No. 6. Washington, DC: National Academy on an Aging Society. http://www.agingsociety.org/agingsociety/pdf/diabetes.pdf (accessed March 23, 2011).

National Center for Health Statistics. 2006. *Health, United States, 2006.* Hyattsville, MD: National Center for Health Statistics. http://www.cdc.gov/nchs/data/hus/hus06.pdf (accessed March 23, 2011).

———. 2009a. "Deaths: Final Data for 2006." *National Vital Statistics Reports* 57(14): 1–136. http://www.cdc.gov/nchs/data/nvsr/nvsr57/nvsr57_14.pdf (accessed March 25, 2011).

———. 2009b. *Health, United States, 2009.* Hyattsville, MD: National Center for Health Statistics. http://www.cdc.gov/nchs/data/hus/hus09.pdf (accessed March 23, 2011).

National Institute for Occupational Safety and Health (NIOSH). 1999. "Stress . . . at Work." NIOSH Publication No. 99-101. Cincinnati, OH: National Institute for Occupational Safety and Health. http://www.cdc.gov/niosh/docs/99-101 (accessed March 23, 2011).

Office of the Superintendent of Financial Institutions Canada. 2007. "Optimal Funding of the Canada Pension Plan." Actuarial Study No. 6. Ottawa: Office of the Superintendent of Financial Institutions Canada. http://www.osfi-bsif.gc.ca/app/DocRepository/1/eng/oca/studies/Optimal_Funding_CPP_e.pdf (accessed February 3, 2011).

Olsen, Kelly A., and Don Hoffmeyer. 2002. "Social Security's Special Minimum Benefit." *Social Security Bulletin* 64(2): 1–15.

Olshansky, S. Jay, Douglas J. Passaro, Ronald C. Hershow, Jennifer Layden, Bruce A. Carnes, Jacob Brody, Leonard Hayflick, Robert N. Butler, David B. Allison, and David S. Ludwig. 2005. "A Potential Decline in Life Expectancy in the United States in the 21st Century." *New England Journal of Medicine* 352(11): 1138–1145.

Organisation for Economic Co-operation and Development (OECD). 2008. *Complementary and Private Pensions thoughout the World 2008.* Paris: Organisation for Economic Co-operation and Development.

Oster, Christopher. 2003. "Good News! Insurers Extend Your Lifespan." *Wall Street Journal*, June 24, D:1.

Palmer, Edward. 2000. "The Swedish Pension Reform Model: Framework and Issues." Social Protection Discussion Paper No. 0012. Washington, DC: World Bank. http://siteresources.worldbank.org/SOCIALPROTECTION/Resources/SP-Discussion-papers/Pensions-DP/0012.pdf (accessed March 24, 2011).

Panis, Constantijn, Michael Hurd, David Loughran, Julie Zissimopoulos, Steven Haider, and Patricia StClair. 2002. *The Effects of Changing Social Security Administration's Early Entitlement Age and the Normal Retirement Age.* Santa Monica, CA: RAND.

Penner, Rudolph G., Pamela Perun, and C. Eugene Steuerle. 2002. *Legal and Institutional Impediments to Partial Retirement and Part-Time Work by Older Workers*. Washington, DC: Urban Institute.

———. 2007. "Letting Older Workers Work." In *Work Options for Older Americans,* Teresa Ghilarducci and John A. Turner, eds. Notre Dame, IN: University of Notre Dame Press, pp. 125–163.

Penner, Rudolph G., and C. Eugene Steuerle. 2007. *Stabilizing Future Fiscal Policy: It's Time to Pull the Trigger*. Washington, DC: Urban Institute. http://www.urban.org/UploadedPDF/411524_future_fiscal_policy.pdf (accessed February 1, 2011).

Pensions Advisory Service. 2008. "TPAS Launches Internet Annuity Planner." News release, May 2. London: Pensions Advisory Service. http://www.pensionsadvisoryservice.org.uk/press-releases/2008/may/tpas-launches-internet-annuity-planner?textSize=small (accessed March 24, 2011).

Pensions Commission. 2005. *A New Pension Settlement for the Twenty-First Century: The Second Report of the Pensions Commission*. London: Stationery Office.

Pensions Policy Institute. 2007. *The Changing Landscape for Private Sector Defined Benefit Pension Schemes*. London: Pensions Policy Institute. http://www.pensionspolicyinstitute.org.uk/uploadeddocuments/PPI_Landscape_for_DB_Schemes_8_October_2007.pdf (accessed March 24, 2011).

Pfau, Wade D. 2008. "Assessing the Applicability of Hypothetical Workers for Defined-Contribution Pensions." GRIPS Policy Information Center Discussion Paper No. 07-11. Tokyo: National Graduate Institute for Policy Studies.

Plumridge, Hester. 2010. "BMW Drives New-Age Hopes for Pensions." *Wall Street Journal,* February 22. http://online.wsj.com/article/SB10001424052748704454304575081783318426578.html?mod=WSJ-Markets-LEFTTopNews (accessed March 24, 2011).

President's Commission to Strengthen Social Security. 2001. *Strengthening Social Security and Creating Personal Wealth for All Americans*. Washington, DC: President's Commission to Strengthen Social Security.

Preston, Samuel H. 2005. "Deadweight?—The Influence of Obesity on Longevity." *New England Journal of Medicine* 352(11): 1135–1137.

Purcell, Patrick J. 2002. *Older Workers: Employment and Retirement Trends*. CRS Report for Congress. Washington, DC: Congressional Research Service.

Quinn, Joseph F. 1999. "Retirement Patterns and Bridge Jobs in the 1990s." EBRI Issue Brief. Washington, DC: Employee Benefit Research Institute.

Retirement USA. 2010. *The Retirement Income Deficit*. Washington, DC: Retirement USA, Pension Rights Center. http://www.retirement-usa.org/retirement-income-deficit-0 (accessed March 24, 2011).

Robinson, Kristen. 2007. *Trends in Health Status and Health Care Use among Older Women*. Trends in Health and Aging Series, No. 7. Hyattsville, MD: National Center for Health Statistics. http://www.cdc.gov/nchs/data/ahcd/agingtrends/07olderwomen.pdf (accessed March 28, 2011).

Rossingh, Danielle. 2004. "Dutch Employers Group Warns over Pre-Pensions." *Investment and Pensions Europe,* November 25. http://ipe.com/articles/print.php?id=10195 (accessed April 19, 2011).

Sakamoto, Junichi. 2005. "Japan's Pension Reform." Social Protection Discussion Paper No. 0541. Washington, DC: World Bank. http://siteresources.worldbank.org/SOCIALPROTECTION/Resources/SP-Discussion-papers/Pensions-DP/0541.pdf (accessed March 24, 2011).

———. 2008. "Roles of the Social Security Pension Schemes and the Minimum Benefit Level under the Automatic Balancing Mechanism." NRI Paper No. 125. Tokyo: Nomura Research Institute. http://www.actuaries.org/Boston2008/Papers/IPM4_Sakamoto.pdf (accessed March 24, 2011).

Sarney, Mark. 2008. "Distributional Effects of Increasing the Benefit Computation Period." Social Security Policy Brief No. 2008-02. Washington, DC: Social Security Administration. http://www.socialsecurity.gov/policy/docs/policybriefs/pb2008-02.pdf (accessed March 24, 2011).

Scherman, Karl Gustaf. 2007. "The Swedish NDC System—A Critical Assessment." Paper presented at the Second Colloquium of the Pension, Benefits, and Social Security Section of the International Actuarial Association, held in Helsinki, Finland, May 21–23. http://www.actuaries.org/PBSS/Colloquia/Helsinki/Papers/Scherman.pdf (accessed March 24, 2011).

Schoeni, Robert F., Vicki A. Freedman, and Robert B. Wallace. 2001. "Persistent, Consistent, Widespread, and Robust? Another Look at Recent Trends in Old-Age Disability." *Journal of Gerontology: Series B: Psychological Sciences and Social Sciences* 56(4): S206–S218.

Sedensky, Matt. 2008. "Study: Bankruptcies Soar for Senior Citizens." Associated Press, August 27. http://www.msnbc.msn.com/id/26427259/ns/business-your_retirement (accessed March 24, 2011).

Segal Company. 2003. *IRS Issues Final Regulations on ERISA Section 204(h) Notices of Reductions in Future Pension Benefits*. New York: Segal Company. http://www.sibson.com/uploads/fd94f605b39349207dafc82aca96bd3.pdf (accessed March 24, 2011).

Shelton, Alison. 2008. *Reform Options for Social Security*. Washington, DC: AARP Public Policy Institute. http://assets.aarp.org/rgcenter/econ/i3_reform.pdf (accessed March 24, 2011).

Singh, Gopal K., and Mohammad Siahpush. 2006. "Widening Socioeconomic Inequalities in U.S. Life Expectancy, 1980–2000." *International Journal of Epidemiology* 35(4): 969–979. http://ije.oxfordjournals.org/content/35/4/969.full (accessed March 24, 2011).

Smith, Denise. 2003. *The Older Population in the United States: March 2002.* Current Population Report P20-546. Washington, DC: U.S. Census Bureau. http://www.census.gov/prod/2003pubs/p20-546.pdf (accessed March 25, 2011).

Social Security Administration. 1986. "Increasing the Social Security Retirement Age: Older Workers in Physically Demanding Occupations or Ill Health." *Social Security Bulletin* 49(10): 5–23. http://www.ssa.gov/policy/docs/ssb/v49n10/v49n10p5.pdf (accessed March 24, 2011).

———. 2004. "Chile's Recent Pension Reform, Passed in February, Changes the Way Retirement Annuities Are Sold, Creates a New Type of Annuity, and Makes It Harder to Retire Early." *International Update: Recent Developments in Foreign Public and Private Pensions.* March issue of newsletter, pp. 2–3. http://www.ssa.gov/policy/docs/progdesc/intl_update/2004-03/2004-03.pdf (accessed March 24, 2011).

———. 2006. *Income of the Population 55 or Older, 2004.* Washington, DC: Social Security Administration. http://www.ssa.gov/policy/docs/statcomps/income_pop55/2004/index.html (accessed March 24, 2011).

———. 2007. "Effective January 1, 2007, Spain's New Income Tax Law Reduces Occupational Pension Tax Incentives for Both Employers and Employees." *International Update: Recent Developments in Foreign Public and Private Pensions.* February issue of newsletter, p. 2. http://www.socialsecurity.gov/policy/docs/progdesc/intl_update/2007-02/2007-02.pdf (accessed March 24, 2011).

Social Security Advisory Board. 2005. *Social Security: Why Action Should Be Taken Soon.* Washington, DC: Social Security Advisory Board. http://www.ssab.gov/documents/WhyActionShouldbeTakenSoon.pdf (accessed March 25, 2011).

Social Security Board of Trustees. 2008. *The 2008 Annual Report of the Board of Trustees of the Federal Old-Age and Survivors Insurance and Federal Disability Insurance Trust Funds.* House Document 110-104. Washington, DC: Social Security Board of Trustees.

———. 2011. *The 2011 Annual Report of the Board of Trustees of the Federal Old-Age and Survivors Insurance and Federal Disability Insurance Trust Funds.* Washington, DC: Social Security Board of Trustees. http://www.socialsecurity.gov/OACT/TR/2011/tr2011.pdf (accessed May 17, 2011).

Society of Actuaries. 2003. *2001 Retirement Risk Survey: Key Findings and Issues.* Schaumburg, IL: Society of Actuaries. http://www.soa.org/files/pdf/rrs_findings.pdf (accessed March 30, 2011).

Soldo, Beth J., Olivia S. Mitchell, Rania Tfaily, and John F. McCabe. 2006. "Cross-Cohort Differences in Health on the Verge of Retirement." NBER Working Paper No. 12762. Cambridge, MA: National Bureau of Economic Research.

Spillman, Brenda C. 2003. *Changes in Elderly Disability Rates and the Implications for Health Care Utilization and Cost.* Washington, DC: U.S. Department of Health and Human Services, Office of the Assistant Secretary for Planning and Evaluation. http://aspe.hhs.gov/daltcp/reports/hcutlcst .htm#exhibit2a (accessed March 25, 2011).

Spiteri, Sharon. 2003. "EU Civil Servants Pension Reform Gets Go-Ahead." *EUobserver,* September 20. http://unpan1.un.org/intradoc/groups/public/ documents/un/unpan014272.htm#CSEEU02 (accessed March 25, 2011).

Steuerle, C. Eugene, Christopher Spiro, and Richard W. Johnson. 1999. *Can Americans Work Longer?* Straight Talk on Social Security and Retirement Policy Series, No. 5. Washington, DC: Urban Institute.

Sundén, Annika. 2009. "The Swedish Pension System and the Economic Crisis." CCR Issue in Brief 9-25. Chestnut Hill, MA: Center for Retirement Research at Boston College.

Swedish Ministry of Health and Social Affairs. 2005. *The Swedish National Strategy Report on Adequate and Sustainable Pensions.* Stockholm: Swedish Ministry of Health and Social Affairs.

Swedish Social Insurance Agency. 2005. *The Swedish Pension System Annual Report 2004.* Stockholm: Swedish Social Insurance Agency.

Takayama, Noriyuki. 2006. "Reforming Social Security in Japan: Is NDC the Answer?" In *Pension Reform: Issues and Prospects for Non-Financial Defined Contribution (NDC) Schemes,* Robert Holzmann and Edward Palmer, eds. Washington, DC: World Bank, pp. 639–647.

Technical Panel on Assumptions and Methods. 2003. *Report to the Social Security Advisory Board.* Washington, DC: U.S. Government Printing Office.

Toft, Christian. 2007. *The Transformation of the German Public Pension System and the Future Pension Benefit Level.* Helsinki: World Institute of Development Economics Research.

Tucker, Larry A., and Glenn M. Friedman. 1998. "Obesity and Absenteeism: An Epidemiologic Study of 10,825 Employed Adults." *American Journal of Health Promotion* 12(3): 202–207.

Turner, John A. 1984. "Population Age Structure and the Size of Social Security." *Southern Economic Journal* 50(4): 1131–1146.

———. 2007. "Social Security Pensionable Ages in OECD Countries: 1949–2035." *International Social Security Review* 60(1): 81–99.

———. 2009. *Social Security Financing: Automatic Adjustments to Restore Solvency.* Washington, DC: AARP Public Policy Institute.

———. 2010a. "Political Risk with Automatic Adjustment Mechanisms for Social Security: Is 'Automatic' Really Automatic?" Paper presented at the International Social Security Association's Sixth International Policy and Research Conference on Social Security, held in Luxembourg, September 29–October 1.

———. 2010b. "Why Don't People Annuitize? The Role of Advice Provided by Retirement Planning Software." Pension Research Council Working Paper No. 2010-07. Philadelphia: Pension Research Council, Wharton School of the University of Pennsylvania.

Turner, John A., and Roy Guenther. 2005. "A Comparison of Early Retirement Pensions in the United States and Russia: The Pensions of Musicians." *Journal of Aging and Social Policy* 17(4): 61–74.

Turner, John A., and Satyendra Verma. 2007. "Why Some Workers Don't Take 401(k) Plan Offers: Inertia versus Economics." CeRP Working Paper 56/07. Turin, Italy: Center for Research on Pensions and Welfare Policies.

Turner, John A., and Hazel A. Witte. 2009. *Retirement Planning Software and Post-Retirement Risks*. Report for the Society of Actuaries and the Actuarial Foundation. Schaumburg, IL: Society of Actuaries. http://www.soa.org/files/pdf/research-pen-retire-planning-soft.pdf (accessed March 25, 2011).

University of California. 2010. *Executive Summary: The Report of the President's Task Force on Post-Employment Benefits, July 2010*. Oakland, CA: University of California Office of the President. http://universityofcalifornia.edu/sites/ucrpfuture/files/2010/08/peb_taskforce_summary_082510.pdf (accessed March 25, 2011).

U.S. Census Bureau. 2010. *Poverty Thresholds 2004*. http://www.census.gov/hhes/www/poverty/data/threshld/thresh04.html (accessed March 25, 2011).

Waldron, Hilary. 2007. "Trends in Mortality Differentials and Life Expectancy for Male Social Security–Covered Workers, by Socioeconomic Status." *Social Security Bulletin* 67(3): 1–28. http://www.ssa.gov/policy/docs/ssb/v67n3/v67n3p1.pdf (accessed March 25, 2011).

Watson Wyatt Worldwide. 2003. "New Pension Law in Belgium." Global News Briefs, May 9. Arlington, VA: Watson Wyatt Worldwide.

———. 2007. "United Kingdom: Pensions Bill Published." News release, January. http://www.watsonwyatt.com/news/media/UK2.pdf (accessed March 25, 2011).

Webb, Anthony, Guan Gong, and Wei Sun. 2007. "An Annuity That People Might Actually Buy." CRR Issue in Brief No. 7-10. Chestnut Hill, MA: Center for Retirement Research at Boston College. http://crr.bc.edu/images/stories/Briefs/ib_7-10.pdf (accessed March 25, 2011).

White, David. 2003. "Employers Support Moves to More Compulsion in Pensions." *Investment and Pensions Europe,* June 3. http://www.ipe.com/news/employers-support-moves-to-more-compulsion-in-pensions_7218.php (accessed March 25, 2011).

Whitehouse, Edward. 2007a. "Life-Expectancy Risk and Pensions: Who Bears the Burden?" OECD Social, Employment, and Migration Working Paper No. 60. Paris: Organisation for Economic Co-operation and Development.

————. 2007b. *Pensions Panorama: Retirement-Income Systems in 53 Countries*. Washington, DC: World Bank.

Whitman, Debra, and Patrick Purcell. 2006. "Topics in Aging: Income and Poverty among Older Americans in 2005." CRS Reports and Issue Briefs Paper No. 23. Washington, DC: Congressional Research Service. http://digitalcommons.ilr.cornell.edu/cgi/viewcontent.cgi?article=1022&context=crs (accessed March 25, 2011).

Zhivan, Natalia A., Stephen A. Sass, Margarita Sapozhnikov, and Kelly Haverstick. 2008. "An 'Elastic' Earliest Eligibility Age for Social Security." CRR Issue in Brief No. 8-2. Chestnut Hill, MA: Center for Retirement Research at Boston College.

# The Author

John A. Turner is director of the Pension Policy Center in Washington, D.C. Previously, he worked at the AARP Public Policy Institute in Washington and at the International Labour Office in Geneva, Switzerland. He has also worked in research offices at the U.S. Social Security Administration and at the U.S. Department of Labor, where he was deputy director of the pension research office for nine years. He has taught as an adjunct lecturer at George Washington University. Turner has published 12 books—two have been translated into Japanese and two are required reading for Society of Actuaries examinations. He has published more than 100 articles. Turner holds a PhD in economics from the University of Chicago.

# Index

The italic letters *n* and *t* following a page number indicate that the subject information of the heading is within a note or table, respectively, on that page. Double italics indicate multiple but consecutive elements.

# About the Institute

The W.E. Upjohn Institute for Employment Research is a nonprofit research organization devoted to finding and promoting solutions to employment-related problems at the national, state, and local levels. It is an activity of the W.E. Upjohn Unemployment Trustee Corporation, which was established in 1932 to administer a fund set aside by Dr. W.E. Upjohn, founder of The Upjohn Company, to seek ways to counteract the loss of employment income during economic downturns.

The Institute is funded largely by income from the W.E. Upjohn Unemployment Trust, supplemented by outside grants, contracts, and sales of publications. Activities of the Institute comprise the following elements: 1) a research program conducted by a resident staff of professional social scientists; 2) a competitive grant program, which expands and complements the internal research program by providing financial support to researchers outside the Institute; 3) a publications program, which provides the major vehicle for disseminating the research of staff and grantees, as well as other selected works in the field; and 4) an Employment Management Services division, which manages most of the publicly funded employment and training programs in the local area.

The broad objectives of the Institute's research, grant, and publication programs are to 1) promote scholarship and experimentation on issues of public and private employment and unemployment policy, and 2) make knowledge and scholarship relevant and useful to policymakers in their pursuit of solutions to employment and unemployment problems.

Current areas of concentration for these programs include causes, consequences, and measures to alleviate unemployment; social insurance and income maintenance programs; compensation; workforce quality; work arrangements; family labor issues; labor-management relations; and regional economic development and local labor markets.